Yours Sincerely

Angela Macnamara

ANGELA
MACNAMARA

VERITAS

Published 2003 by
Veritas Publications
7/8 Lower Abbey Street
Dublin 1
Email publications@veritas.ie
Website www.veritas.ie

ISBN 1 85390 700 6

10 9 8 7 6 5 4 3 2 1

A catalogue record for this book is available from the British Library.

Cover design by Faye Keegan
Printed in the Republic of Ireland by Betaprint Ltd, Dublin

Veritas books are printed on paper made from the wood pulp of managed forests.
For every tree felled, at least one tree is planted, thereby renewing natural resources.

*The spiritual life is contained in the most
simple experiences of everyday living.*

(Henri Nouwen)

Contents

Introduction

From the many snatches of people's lives which I have been especially privileged to share I know that no one needs to do magnificent things or travel to amazing places in order to have a unique story to tell. What matters is to allow and enjoy the free-fall that is life. It is good for adults to return to being the inventive and imaginative child who has a whole page of paper to fill up with whatever shapes and splotches of colour come freely to mind. We should allow ourselves to follow our dream or intuition without inhibition and without fear of criticism. It's okay that nothing we have ever done is fully accepted by everyone. That's normal.

Not all of us can climb Mount Everest or swim the Channel. Few of us have the courage or opportunity to travel across the world to dig wells in the desert, care for starving people, or rescue street-children. Wonderful people do such things.

But for many of us there are quieter ways of making our contribution to life. We all get promptings. For me there was the 1960s thought that young people should know more than I had done about marriage and family life. I followed the prompting to share with schoolgirls and see how it worked. Later, quite unexpectedly, what is called an 'Agony Column' in the *Sunday Press* became my lot. The mountain of letters I received from readers became my Everest and, as Ireland changed, I struggled to find a foothold. I wrote about fifty letters a week. The objective was not an ego trip for me, but simply to offer a hearing ear and a friendly response. An average of three questions and answers were published weekly in the column. The rest went to people who had sent stamp-addressed envelopes, and still the pile grew. Many were anonymous, so regretfully, I could not find a way to reach them.

I continued the talks in schools, sharing with teenagers the thrills and spills of becoming an adult. Over time I met thousands of children, younger ones every few years, and their parents all over the country. Groups I was invited to share with were in schools, clubs, parish halls, churches and private homes and ranged in numbers from ten to two thousand at a 'go'. (But of course, if you prepare well you can talk as well to two thousand as you can to ten). I learnt so much about the changing Ireland through letters and face-to-face.

Working with children has allowed the child in me to emerge. It's great to explore and experience our multi-faceted selves and to give each facet its open day: this is the serious me, this is the whimsical me, then comes the spiritual self, the funny self and now the dreams. Lao-Tzu, the great Chinese philosopher, wrote 'when you are content to be simply yourself and don't compare or compete, everybody will respect you.'

It is quite remarkable to note how the Ireland into which I was born, educated, married and worked has changed. From the religious fervour of the Eucharistic Congress (1932) to the year 2002 must go down in history as an era of swings and roundabouts. The Celtic Tiger crouched in the undergrowth arriving with an explosion creating a helter-skelter and then departed leaving everyone up in the air.

At any age and in any conditions, the sensual feeling of creativity can make life a celebration. Too seldom have I allowed myself to run barefoot on the dewy lawn. But one June morning I did so, wearing my night-dress. Peter and I enjoyed that early morning spree so much. Spontaneous little movements of the spirit can be more memorable than an expensive dinner at the Ritz or coming face-to-face with the Celtic Tiger. 'Don't be too easily tamed', I realised in my older age, having had to overcome my own taming. There were times when I had been afraid to laugh too loudly, weep too publicly, express myself too forthrightly. And then I began to change. I broke into poetry: creativity is an act of cherishing an experience.

Mighty Love

Wisp on wisp of cloud and mist,
Swooping swallow, diving fish on
Water stilled, fly-flitted green
'Neath heathered mountains peaking clean.
And from the depths as from above
All are maintained by Mighty Love.

Breath of breeze through spring-laced trees,
Bowers of flowers, perfumed sweet,
Spider spins at cobweb silk,
Cattle drowsy, warm with milk.
And from the depths as from above
All are maintained by Mighty Love.

Sun rises shy, dawn pinks grey sky,
Wide stretching child and yawning man,
Shutters shudder, doors ajar
Brash cities wake to people power.
And from the depths as from above
All are maintained by Mighty Love.

Unless I had taken out pen and paper I would not have enjoyed giving the best I could to that lovely morning. No matter that it isn't a masterpiece; 'There is no absolute standard of beauty' (JK Galbraith).

Where did it all begin for me, you may wonder. Come with me, I shall enjoy our journeying together.

1
My Kind of Childhood

My kind of early childhood will never be seen again. So let me share with you something of its antique flavour.

I arrived into the world at a most inopportune time. It was 16 October 1931. My parents, George Little and Alice Mulhern-Little, were moving house on that day. Their move was later than planned and my birth was earlier.

Our house was a large, double-fronted Victorian house on Rathgar Road in Dublin. Wide granite steps led to the hall door. A slope for the pram and some steps led to the side entrance. The No. 15 trams rattled up and down the road travelling from the terminus in Terenure to Nelson's Pillar in the city centre. Beyond Terenure the countryside began. Indeed, in later years we went for picnics by the fields, streams and woods of Tallaght.

But on that October day in 1931, while the removal men were heaving the furniture into our new house my mother was labouring in the nursing home. My father raced between both. Friends helped. I arrived safely and soundly, as did the furniture. But there were many things stacked away in drawers and presses which my mother took a long time to discover. In later years I remember her saying 'I still don't know what's buried in those top presses in the pantry, maybe the yellow jug or the jelly mould are there?' We children occasionally climbed up on chairs in the cool, flagged pantry and poked in the back of the presses. A sturdy fridge was bought so that the milk would be kept fresh for me and my sister Mary, who was two and a half years older. Mother got 'Grade A' milk, which was rich and creamy. Indeed, 'top of the bottle' was used as cream to pour on porridge and desserts. For many years I thought the milk had the unattractive name of 'Grey Day'. Yet those were bright, carefree days remembered for innocent events like a large glass of cold, creamy milk enjoyed under the trees on a warm summer's day, or hot chocolate by the nursery fire in winter.

For an imaginative little girl as I was there were fears as well as high delights. The story was told at home that Mary and I went with our parents to the play of *Peter Pan*. I must have been about four as I sat or knelt on Daddy's knee for a good part of the play. It seems that I looked over his shoulder towards the back of the auditorium for quite some time during the performance. Daddy whispered 'Look this way, see the pirates coming to find Peter Pan.' But I continued to look in the opposite direction. When Daddy asked me why I was looking in that direction, I whispered, 'Because they might come up from behind us.'

The Eucharistic Congress, led by a Papal Cardinal Legate brought great celebration, ceremony and devotion to Dublin when I was one year old. The country was *en fête*. I have seen the photographs of our house bedecked with flags. It was a huge event, since the vast majority of Irish people were ardent Catholics in those years. Flags fluttered and bunting danced in all the little roads and streets of the city.

Daddy had his thriving medical practice at home. He was also a keen historian and writer. So we had to be quiet and unobtrusive. But we had a large, bright nursery where we played on bad weather days. A coal fire burned there in winter with a sturdy, black iron fire-guard. Daddy had a bath installed in the corner of the nursery. It had a hinged lid, which closed down providing us with a play-counter when bath-time was over and we had been dried before the fire.

We never played in front of the house, but we had a grand back garden. The house had been a private school before my parents bought it, so there was a hedge-surrounded tennis court. This doubled as a croquet lawn at times. At the far end there was a pavilion, which had been erected for the schoolchildren's indoor recreation and gym. It was a lovely garden playroom for us, even having a fireplace for chilly days. Table tennis was installed there as we grew older. Outside the pavilion Daddy got a play area made with a swing, seesaw and trapeze. That area was surrounded by fruit trees, which I remember being magical in early summer with their pink and white blossom. High granite walls with creepers, occasional shrubs and flowers surrounded the garden. We never saw our adult neighbours from garden level.

There was also an adults' area in the garden. It had a teahouse facing a lawn of rosebeds. This little area was known as 'Daddy's Grass'. There was no messing around there as he prized his lovely roses. Summer lunch and tea were often in the teahouse, which I remember as smelling of warm wood and wicker chairs. It had in it a bell connected with the kitchen so that the maid could be called if anything was needed for the meal.

Those were the post-Victorian years when domestic help was still easily available. Our home was something of a hang-over from the upstairs/downstairs homes of the previous generation. Indeed, later as a schoolgirl, I thought that our household was old-fashioned and it made me uneasy about bringing friends in. Our drawing-room seemed to me to be like a museum because it had so many *objets d'art* collected by Daddy over the years. It was a fine room stretching from the front to the back of the house. At the garden end there were French doors leading to a wrought-iron platform and steps to the garden. No one played running or jumping games in the drawing-room; it was for gracious living.

Our paternal grandfather, Papa, lived with us from the early years when his wife died. Daddy ruled the roost with kind but no-nonsense strictness and discipline. My quiet and gentle mother bowed to his authority. She had her role as mistress of the house and mother, but was without power in the wider decision-making. She oversaw the kitchen staff, which consisted in my childhood of a nanny, a cook, a houseman and – on Mondays – Elsie who came in to do the huge wash. We chatted with Elsie as she carried large baskets of newly-washed clothes to hang out in the yard at the bottom of the garden. She was a smiling woman in a navy flowered crossover overall, pink cheeks and red hands from constant contact with the wash-board and hot, soapy water. The gardener was overseen by 'the doctor'. We liked all the staff and they seemed to like us. The maids were happy. Gusts of laughter could be heard from the kitchen at times. We were fond of them and sorry when they left after many years of service. Daddy also had a secretary, a lovely young woman whom I greatly admired as she took enthusiastic interest in little school events that I shared with her from time to time later on. Over a few years, domestic help became harder to get and, rightly, more expensive.

Mary and I didn't go to primary school. We had a governess, Miss O'Riordan, who came to teach us at home. In summer we had classes with her in the pavilion. The table was beside one of the rose-surrounded windows overlooking the 'children's garden.' It was quiet and warm, flies and an occasional bee buzzed in the raftered ceiling and birds twittered in the trees and shrubs outside. Miss O'Riordan was a kind, gentle, arthritic lady. Sometimes we hid from her as she came out to the garden to collect us for classes. We climbed trees and looked down at her as she called 'Máire! Aingeal!' She taught us through Irish. I was about three when I started classes, but Mary had been taught for a year before I started.

Sometimes I escaped from lessons at about 11 a.m. when I knew that Papa would be home from Mass and at his breakfast. I knew that he would give me fingers of toast and marmalade. He called me 'Skinny-bones'. Even though he was strict, he and I had a soft spot for one another. Nanny would wash my sticky fingers and I would run back through the garden to class. In the afternoons Nanny (Lily) brought us for a regular walk and home to tea in the nursery. We often had a couple of pennies for a treat in The Rathgar

Sweeteries. The lady there had a trayful of penny specials. We were not indulged; when a treat was over, that was the end.

By the age of five I was ready for first First Holy Communion and my mother brought me into Mother St Barbara in the convent of Marie Reparatrice, Merrion Square, who prepared me for this great occasion. Mary had been with her the previous year. I was then able to read my little prayer book. Mary's dress was altered for me. My mother didn't believe in emphasising the dress aspect. There was no question of our being given money by relations or friends. Mum gave me a lovely, comforting and serene outlook on Holy Communion. I still remember that day as having a quality of happiness about it that was never repeated. In the afternoon we visited the Carmelite Monastery in Delgany where Mum had a nun friend. I remember going to Fr Hurley in Rathgar for my First Confession and telling him my worst sin: I had stolen grapes from Papa's room. Fr Hurley was really kind. I loved confession and the feeling of saying 'Sorry' to God, His wiping the slate clean and starting anew. We had slates in the nursery, so I understood that idea well.

It seems that when I was about three Fr Hurley was visiting our home shortly before my birthday. He asked me what present I would like and I replied, 'A corset'. The adults were mightily surprised. It seems that Lily, our nanny, who slept with us in the nursery, made a jingling sort of noise when she was dressing in the dim morning light. I had asked her later what the noise was. She told me that it was her corset. I wore nothing that made a jingly noise, so that decided me.

Mary and I played together during those early years. We seldom had other children in to play. Only now and again did we join our cousins for parties. Rathgar Road was a busy road and the neighbours next door were older people. There were no children in adjacent houses. We played house and hospital, mummies and babies, shop and dressing-up. We climbed the apple trees and jumped from the upper branches, did acrobatics on the swing, rode our bicycles and enjoyed all the creative games happily. We didn't miss other children since we had never experienced play in larger groups.

I remember one day when Mummy got us ready for a party. We wore organdie dresses, puff-sleeved and hand-painted around the hems, which an old family friend had made for us. White socks and shoes were part of the outfits, little gold bracelets on brown arms. We were waiting in the garden for Mummy to call us when she was ready. We had wandered to the yard where there was a rain-water barrel beside the greenhouse. We got two sticks and began to 'fish' bringing up all sorts of weed and soggy leaves from the depths of the barrel. Can you imagine what those organdie dresses were like when, in a matter of minutes, Mummy called us?

In that same yard, at an older age, we collected red, juicy apples from a neighbour's tree that leaned into our garden. Daddy had made it clear that we could only have the apples from branches that reached into our garden. I remember sitting high up on the wall measuring the branches with a ruler to be sure that the apples were really ours. Those apples always seemed to be more interesting than our own! In the Ireland I grew up in we learned a lot about conscience and sin, but Mummy softened any harsh-seeming message by telling us of the love of God which was the motivating force in her life. 'You are so special to God', she used to reassure me. So she made that truth the mainstay of my life as well as of hers.

2

A Light Goes On and Off

A son is born. My parents were overjoyed by the arrival of David when I was about three years old and Mary was five. David was a beautiful, healthy, curly-headed little boy. He thrived.

One day, when David was two, my mother and we three children set out for an afternoon with Granny. She lived in Donnybrook and we often went to her on Nanny's half-day. As usual we played in her garden if it was fine and upstairs in the study on the cold or wet days. This was a brisk, dry day. Nell, Granny's long-time home help, gave us lemonade and biscuits while the adults had tea in the drawing-room. We joined them after tea. In those days children played on their own while the adults enjoyed a quiet chat. Mum was telling Granny about plans for David's forthcoming birthday.

When we arrived home Mum parked her car on the side of the road opposite our house and guided the three of us across the road. Daddy was in his consulting room with a family friend and they waved from the window. Daddy was wearing the white linen coat he wore during consulting hours. We proceeded down to the side door, which Maggie, the cook, opened for us. It seems that David made a sudden decision to turn back as though making for the car. He raced out the gate.

Suddenly I heard the shrieking of brakes and a thud. I looked back and saw Daddy running down the steps towards the road.

Mum had gone out the gate. Within a minute Daddy was coming
back in and all I saw was that he held David in his arms and my
father's white coat was covered with blood. Maggie rushed Mary
and I ahead of her into the house. She brought us to the
downstairs study and told us to stay there until she came back.

We were silent. I seem to remember walking around the room
in circles. Then there is a blank. The next thing I remember is
being in my bed and Mum kneeling beside me telling me that
David had gone to God. Even still, I can only suppose that that was
next morning because subsequently I was told that David had
been rushed to hospital and operated on immediately. Daddy was
at the operation when his little son died. It seems that Mary and I
were brought over to Granny's to stay for some days. I seem to
recall the stay in Granny's in isolation from the accident. Only
years afterwards did we see photographs of the horse-driven
hearse carrying the tiny white coffin. The horses had white
plumes on their heads instead of the usual black.

The shock was so great for me at the age of five that I seem
only to have memories like scattered snapshots of parts of the
tragedy. But a curious memory troubled me for years: the
Christmas before David's accident, he and Mary and I were playing
Santa Claus in the nursery. We had a draught screen and the one
behind it had a turn at being Santa. 'Santa' wrapped the 'gifts'
roughly in old paper and we came in turn to receive them. Then
there was a new Santa. In the first round Mary gave me the
familiar hairbrush, which I unwrapped excitedly and saw it as
though for the first time. Then David was Santa. He gave me my
parcel – the hairbrush again. Disappointed by this I turned back
and hit him on the head with the brush. Of course he roared.
Nanny said crossly to me 'You're very bold; you could have killed
him.' Somehow after David's death I kept remembering this and
wondering if I had anything to do with what had happened. I
didn't tell anyone.

Interestingly, even as an adult I never brought myself to talk to
either of my parents about this tragedy. It must have been so awful

for them. It was never mentioned before us children at home. What a suffering for parents is the loss of a child. It was years before Mary and I were allowed out on to Rathgar Road without an adult.

Mary was nine and I seven before we went to 'big school'. That was the Convent of the Sacred Heart in Leeson Street, which my mother had attended as a girl. She was head-girl there in her last year. What a shock I found it. I had never before come across so many children milling around together. I felt lost and frightened. Since then I have never liked milling crowds. The thing I wanted most was to have that mysterious person they called 'a friend'. But I didn't know how to get one. I pushed that hope even further away when at one of the first Irish classes the teacher asked if anyone remembered an Irish poem from the previous year. No-one responded so at last I said that I did. I told her that it was 'Croppaí Bocht' and I proceeded to the top of the classroom as we had always done for Miss O'Riordan. I noticed children giving me strange looks, but thought that was because I was new. I began the recitation with actions and particular voices for the mother and child in the poem. By that time the other girls were obviously withholding laughter and nudging each other. Miss Power had to tell them to stop. She encouraged me to keep on to the end. Then she announced that I deserved a clap. They all clapped, but they laughed as well. Soon I learned that when asked to say a poem one simply stood up in one's place and raced or stumbled through the poem. I felt that I had disgraced myself. Why had Miss O'Riordan encouraged those actions and voices? I wished I was 'normal'. I also had a lot of chest colds and teachers allowed me sit close to the lukewarm radiator, the best heat available in the huge classroom in those wartime years. Other girls decided that I was 'teacher's pet'– not a desirable position for one who most wanted to have a friend.

Not many months later I was diagnosed as having a primary TB and had to leave school for a year of illness and quite a lonely time at home. I made the Child Jesus my imaginary friend and chatted away to him. I created a dent in the pillow for him to lie beside me. That began a lifetime of natural conversation with my 'Invisible Companion'. I concluded that year by staying with my much-loved and childless Godparents who lived at the sea-side in Bray, Co. Wicklow. How I loved it there. They had a comfortable old house and two dogs, and we went for adventurous walks on the beach, up Bray Head and into the woods of Kilruddery. They laughingly introduced me to people as their adopted daughter. They had two maids with whom I was on much more familiar terms than I was with the maids at home. They were young and we shared a lot of fun.

I was an avid reader. My Godparents had really old copies of Grimm's fairy stories. They had black and white illustrations of fairies and goblins. Dark woods and turretted castles, kind princesses, and every frog was a possible prince. Along with fairy stories came the school-stories of Angela Brazil and Elinor M. Brent-Dyer. Richmal Crompton's 'William' stories were told with huge humour and William was a comic reflection of daring I admired.

Meanwhile, at home, Mummy gave birth to Frank, my second brother. To have another son must have been a great comfort to my parents. A few years later, when I was nine, the youngest and last child, Leonard, was born. With two of each sex our family was complete and I was ready to go back to school to try again.

3
No Words For It

Sunday lunch in an hotel by the seaside; what could be nicer, I thought as I and my family drove off. Such an outing was a real treat for us. I was about ten years old. We were visiting friends of my parents who were staying there.

Greg and Sylvia (not their real names) had no children of their own and seemed to like having us around. I didn't like Greg: he was a 'Ho, ho, ho!' type of man. When he and I were on our own he tickled me in a way that made me feel very uncomfortable. But I couldn't say that to anyone. 'Tickling is only for fun,' they might say. After the hotel lunch we were all sitting in the garden when Greg asked me if I'd like to see a model ship that was on the upstairs landing of the hotel. I agreed and we sauntered off. The model ship was amazing. Just about eighteen inches long, it had so much detail in the rigging, the little ladders and even the tiny men at their jobs on deck and high up in the masts. I chatted away about it. Greg then told me that their bedroom was on the other side of the landing and would I like to see it. I said 'Yes' and he unlocked the door bringing me into a spacious bedroom with a large window with heavy drapes. He suggested that I sit on the edge of the big billowing bed. He then appeared to be getting something from the wardrobe. I couldn't see him as the wardrobe door was between me and him.

In a couple of minutes he emerged. He was exposing himself and showing me what happens to men when aroused. I was horrified. I felt breathless and sat in terror. I had no idea what was happening. He didn't touch me, but asked me a couple of questions. I had little to say.

Soon we were on our way down to the garden again. We must have passed the model ship, but I didn't see it. Outside the sun was still shining. I went over and sat beside my mother on a garden seat. Mary and our little brother, Frank, were exploring the shrubbery and laughing. Mum prompted me to join them, but I shook my head. The joy of the day had evaporated. I felt cold. For the remainder of the afternoon I was quiet. I could hear 'Ho, ho, ho' from the other side of the lawn. Back home I felt that I couldn't tell anyone; I didn't have any words for the situation. When I tried to go to sleep that night I felt the same cold sense of horror. 'Is my daddy like that?' I wondered. Later, during the holidays, I didn't look at Daddy on the beach. I ran ahead as we all went swimming.

Occasionally Greg and Sylvia invited Mary and me to their house for afternoon tea and a game of cards. When next they did so my mother considered me sulky when I didn't want to go. She insisted that I should go saying that they were very kind to ask us. Did I enjoy the cards? she enquired. Yes, I did. Not wanting to be further questioned, I decided to go. But I was careful and didn't follow the routine where Sylvia and Mary went out to the kitchen to get the dainty tea-tray and heat the scones while Greg amused me. I determined to go with the women. This was commented on, 'Ho, ho, ho,' laughed Greg, 'Are we being shy? Getting domesticated, what? Ho, ho, ho.'
I continued on my determined way to the kitchen.

I was an adult before I told my sister what had happened. She felt as I did about Greg. We both realised that parents should look very closely at a situation where a child suddenly doesn't want to join a certain person or group or, indeed, be with a particular baby-sitter. I well understand what children go through and have been acutely aware of their need to talk about such occurrences. My experience has made me very sensitive to what girls in schools have struggled to tell me on some occasions. Even fifty years later, and with a somewhat more enlightened educational approach to the subject, the same sort of situations exist. I don't recall thinking that I had done anything wrong, but the situation was too strange and frightening even to try to find words to relate. One never forgets. In my adulthood I have gradually become able to understand some of the unresolved issues concerning sexuality that torment certain people. I have felt the need to have compassion. I think we are healed by wanting to forgive the other person. A veil falls between us and remembered pain. It becomes experience to be used positively. Perhaps it is useful that I have never forgotten my feelings as a little girl of ten.

Did such an experience help me in my work with children? I believe it did, just as I believe that all our experiences can bring us to sensitive understanding. Later in life things that have taught us surface and can be used to good ends.

I worked with children for years before any hint of this subject became more openly talked about. I used to touch on it in two ways. The first was in connection with the section of our day that dealt with the physical aspects of the developing bodies of boys and girls. Procreation is such an amazing process that it deserves our greatest respect. We talked about how the sperm and ovum, each such minute particles, join and a unique human life begins. Nowadays the twelve-year-olds take a great interest in the process. I indicate how honoured we are to share with God the capacity for procreation, how we should respect that gift. That brings me to talk about respect for our own bodies and those of other people. It is wrong to abuse another person and to treat their body uncaringly as a plaything. If another person – a young person or an adult – touches you in a rude or crude way you should shout at them to 'Get Lost'. How dare they violate you in that way! You should talk to an adult about what has happened – perhaps to a parent, teacher or counsellor; maybe to an aunt with whom you can talk easily. I assure them that they can talk with me if they have any questions around all that, as well, of course, as all the other different things which they may wish to share. But more of that later.

4

James Announces War

It was James, our houseman, who told me that war had started. It was September 1939 and I was almost eight years old. James and I chatted from time to time as he went about his work. Sometimes he was in the garden. He often wheeled me at a run, on top of the cut grass in the wheelbarrow. I still love the smell of newly-mown grass.

On this particular day he sat at the large kitchen table cleaning silver; pale cutlery was heaped up for shining. But it was while he was putting the cutlery back in the sideboard that he told me. Isn't it strange how we remember such details when associated with news that is startling or shocking to us? I looked at him, 'Where is the war?' I queried. 'It's to be all over Europe,' he replied. 'And will people fight in Ireland?' I asked. He shrugged. 'We're neutral,' he said. 'What's neutral?' I asked. 'We're not supposed to take sides with no-one,' James explained, making his way back to the kitchen. Later James chose to join the British army.

I went out to the garden. I had thought of wars as being only in history books. Miss O'Riordan had told us of ancient wars in Ireland, but to me they were just history. 'Will people die?' I wondered fearfully. I looked around the garden. Everything looked comfortably the same as ever, birds sang, there were apples on the grass, the wheelbarrow was on its end where grass-cuttings had recently been unloaded. These things were suddenly lovely, comforting things. James often joked. I tried to brush from my mind what he had told me.

Shortly after that Daddy appeared one day in an army officer's uniform. He was to be a reserve army doctor, on call in case of emergency. He looked so handsome. But I feared for him and for us.

By 1940 gas masks had been fitted and distributed to the family. Our names were on the boxes, which were stacked under the stairs in the basement. I thought I wouldn't be able to breathe if I wore mine for long. Daddy reassured us. The long, tiled passageway in our basement was to be used as a shelter in case of an air-raid. There was no window leading directly into the basement passageway. A long couch was put there and two electric fires had their flexes extended so that they would reach from the sockets in the breakfast-room and study where they were normally used. There were rugs and cushions and baby Leonard's pram was left there. We were told that if Daddy called us during the night, we were to have slippers and dressing-gowns ready, grab our eiderdowns and come down to the 'passage' (as the basement was known).

I tried not to think about it, but if a car back-fired or there was any loud and unusual sound, I wondered with alarm 'Is this the war?' I had heard the air-raid warnings being practised to familiarise people with their sound. And the 'All Clear' followed. Air-raid shelters were erected in the city centre. I remember seeing these large rectangular 'giant's shoe boxes' in O'Connell Street in the vicinity of the GPO. But they were never used except as 'viewing-points' from the flat roofs of which the local lads viewed any parade or gathering of people for protests. Children from the inner city were said to give one another spontaneous concert performances using these flat roofs as a stage. Happily all the uses were innocent. It was quite some time after the war before these shelters were demolished.

Some individual families built their own 'air-raid shelters' in their gardens, either beehive shape erected by a builder or simply

by digging a hole, putting on a roof of corrugated iron, covering it
with the mound of dug-out soil and topping it with lawn grass.
These became play-houses for the children when the emergency
ended. Erected also were great piles of turf along the roadside in
the Phoenix Park. Our national fuel came into its own in the city at
that time because imported fuel was scarce at first and totally
unavailable as the 1940s progressed. Many families purchased
allotments of bog up the Dublin mountains and dug their own turf
at weekends. Most of the turf was wet for a long time and skill in
building the stacks of turf for storage was of the utmost
importance if it was to dry out sufficiently to be usable. In many
households wet turf was put around the grate, beside a basic fire of
wood so that it would dry sufficiently to be of use in heating the
room. Warm clothes were essential and we wore layers of jumpers.
People sat around these grey, smoking fires wrapped in rugs. There
was a great cheer when fires began to flame. Since electricity was
also rationed, we could only enjoy the occasional luxury of electric
heating.

Everything seemed normal until one night Daddy called us.
ARP men were running up the road calling on people to turn off
their lights. It was like a nightmare at first, but Mary and I got up
and donned slippers and dressing-gowns. Clutching our
eiderdowns we ran to the basement. I remember being squashed
between two others on the couch, petrified. Leonard gurgled in his
pram delighted to be up in the middle of the night. He was an
antidote to my fear. Frank was sleepy and hugged a teddy. The
electric fires were on. My mother smilingly distributed books and
toys and shook Holy Water over us all. That made me feel safer. I
wondered if Granny was all right in her house. She was the one I
seemed to focus on. Michael Kavanagh, a friend of Daddy's, had
been visiting and he was still there. To my horror, he and Daddy
went up to the bathroom window to see what we were told were
the Irish flares being shot up into the night sky from Portobello
barracks to indicate our neutrality to planes, which we believed had
mistaken their destination. I feared for Daddy and Michael upstairs

at the open bathroom window. I imagined a bomb getting in the window. But I just sat still. Mum went to make tea so she, too, disappeared from the passage for a little while returning with biscuits and hot drinks. We heard distant explosions. 'Save Granny,' I prayed. Then came the 'All Clear'. I don't remember anything else about the night, but in the morning my first thought was for Granny. Mum reassured me. All the news was about bombs that fell on the north side of the city. It was assumed that they were dropped by German airmen who had mistaken our country for Great Britain. In Dublin bombs fell on different occasions during 1940–41 at North Circular Road, Phoenix Park, and Sandycove. Also experiencing attack by bombing were Campile in Wexford, Kilmacanogue in Wicklow and Counties Carlow and Louth. The biggest blitz in the thirty-two counties was in Belfast, Northern Ireland. In that attack nearly a thousand people died and more than two and a half thousand were injured. But, as children, we didn't know of all these bombings. Most were at a distance and did not cause emergencies local to our home. We children were not told about them and were not allowed listen to the news on the wireless (as the radio was then called).

Some weekends Daddy went on manoeuvres with army contingents. My mother assured us that he was safe and that the soldiers were simply practising what would be done if the need occurred. I always made for the safety of the house if there was any unexpected crashing or booming sound or if a plane passed over. At night strange-sounding planes often drummed over our house, but since there were no warnings given we grew to accept them even if we awoke to hear them.

Strangely, I don't associate the war with school. I loved school and everything there seemed to be as usual except for the cold classrooms where we were allowed wear our coats. Only faint heat came from the big iron radiators. Our exercise books were made of poor-quality, off-white paper. We said that they were made with porridge-meal. There were even little flakes of 'meal' in the paper.

Those were years of necessary economy. Many things were rationed. There were coupons allotted for foodstuffs and clothing and we took great care of the clothes we had. Mothers darned socks and put false hems on skirts and coats. Men had their suits and shirt collars 'turned' so that the inner good part would replace the worn bit. Sheets were torn down the centre when they got worn and the outside edges machined together making a centre seam. Our kitchen cooker was burning cheap coke, turf and wood – often wet – so there was very little heat. We had a gas stove as well for which there was a gas supply for limited hours only. The little bit of gas available from it during forbidden hours was known as a 'glimmer' and would boil a kettle if left for long enough. There was an inspector who was called the 'Glimmer Man' who could pounce at any time and if your cooker was warm he knew that you had been using the 'glimmer' and he would disconnect you immediately. People said that housewives could bribe him with a nice hot cup of tea! Often if there was tea left over in the teapot after the meal, it was strained into a bowl and reheated for later use. Mothers had to plan all the meals according to what was available in the shops. Bread was dark brown and coarse, but it was possible to do some baking at home – a real treat. Cornflour was used for cake-baking and had a strange, smooth consistency. I liked these cakes, but generally people didn't care for them. Bananas and oranges were unknown to children during the war years and for a few years later because of the scarcity of imported foods of all kinds. I'm sure that, as children, we didn't praise or thank Mum enough for her inventiveness and industry in anticipating everyone's needs in spite of the scarcities. On Sundays after Mass we went to Fitzgerald's sweet shop in Rathgar and each of us chose our quarter pound of sweets for the week. They were all put together in a bag and distributed during the week. There were no other sweets as the coupons ran out quickly.

Hot water was a luxury. There was a copper geyser in our bathroom over the bath; an amazingly moody contraption. It was operated by gas. Turn on the water, ignite the pilot, and back away.

There was then a pop, some angry splutters and great sighing sounds like a giant with bronchitis. The amount and temperature of the water that spouted out varied. Some cold, and then gushes of boiling water. There was no question of being in the bath for all this; no question, either, of having a decently full bath. Just enough to cover the legs fairly well – and don't let the soap fall into the water where it would become soft and slimy, which was so wasteful. It was not done to be really garden-stained from rough and tumble games, another child had to use the same water afterwards. So wash dirty hands and knees at the basin before getting into the bath for an all-over freshen-up. No incentive to relax. Get out quickly. Gas was valuable. I can't imagine what the shower-saturated teenagers of today would have made of the situation.

I wasn't curious about the details of the war. I didn't want to know. Mary tells me now that she wanted to know all that was happening and had to purloin an occasional daily paper and lock herself in the bathroom for a read. Perhaps the two-and-a-half years between us made a difference? I pretended to myself that Ireland was so small that it would be overlooked. Mentally I pushed our little island further out into the sea.

5
Collapse and Insecurity

One morning when I was about twelve, I was yawning and stretching at 'get-up' time when I heard a great thump on the landing outside our bedroom door. I shouted to Mary and we both rushed out to see what it was. Daddy was slumped on the floor. I ran back into our bedroom and sat on my bed shivering violently. Mum was at early Mass. Mary called someone from the kitchen and they tried to get Daddy back to bed. I blocked my ears with shaking hands. Later when my mother arrived. Daddy was brought to hospital. We were told that he had had a heart attack. Once again I feared that he might die. It seemed to me that my relatively carefree childhood ended on that day. From then on we were told to be quiet and not annoy Dad as he was to have tranquil time for recovery. A locum was arranged, but most patients preferred to wait for Dad. I became a peace-at-all-costs person, trying to keep my two small brothers from fighting, shouting, telling tales and messing as all small boys do. 'Daddy might die, Daddy might die' were the words constantly ringing in my ears.

One day I overheard my mother on the 'phone. She was saying 'Yes, but what about money? Where will it come from?' I froze struck by an aspect of the situation I hadn't thought about before. I never spoke of that fear either. Who was there to tell? I became afraid to be alone in a room with Daddy unless others were there. If he even yawned I looked at him anxiously; if he put his head in his hands I left the room. He did have subsequent heart attacks so my anxiety for him continued during my adolescent years. Yet he also got back to work and my mother faithfully drove him on his ' rounds' to patients ever after that. On arriving home from school on my bicycle I always glanced up at their bedroom window. If the blind was fully drawn, I felt myself tighten with fear for someone must be in bed.

One day when I came home from school my mother was by the fire. She had a cough and was staying indoors. We chatted a bit before she again got a bout of coughing. She took out her handkerchief and in a minute it was soaked in blood. I was horrified and wanted to get Daddy. But she said 'No! I don't want to upset him. It will pass.' So I wasn't able to get help. She left the room for a few minutes and came back trying to chat again. I tried to respond brightly, adding, 'Don't talk, Mum, it might only make you cough again.' She laughed it off, reassuring me 'It's only a cold.' But I felt a great sense of fear. It wasn't like the coughs other people got. Some weeks later Daddy got to know of Mum's problem. She went to hospital. I didn't want to go in to see her. I was afraid, so he didn't insist. He later explained that the haemorrhage had a simple enough explanation: years before Mum had her tonsils cauterised which left a weak blood vessel in her throat. This was inclined to burst if she coughed severely. As her cough got better, the throat healed. I prayed so hard if ever Mum got a cold, 'God, please don't let it happen'. More than ever I tried to please them both.

But my school reports were not as good as Daddy wanted. I dreaded the arrival of these. I was going through a giddy patch at school having decided to myself that being serious and good was no way to become popular. True, I was making more friends, but the reports reflected my new distractions. Anyway, well behaved or giddy, I was hopeless at maths and Latin. I had many a nervous journey on the number 15 tram (Terenure–Nelson's Pillar) as I faced into these classes.

One day, before our evening meal I was sitting at the study table ostensibly doing my homework. In fact I was copying the Latin homework of another girl, putting in suitable mistakes so that the copying would not be recognised and yet my Latin would seem to be a bit better. The nun who taught us was so kind. I wanted to please her too. I didn't notice Daddy coming into the room behind me. He looked over my shoulder.

The first thing I heard was that measured, angry question 'What are you doing?' 'Latin,' I told him feeling the blood drain from my face. 'You are copying that exercise,' he accused me. 'I couldn't understand it,' I stammered. 'That is no excuse for cheating,' he said, 'You are a disgrace to the family.' He lifted the other girl's exercise book. We were called in to dinner. Daddy left the room. I sat where I was, in tears. Later someone called me in to dinner. I wiped my eyes and went in. There was silence as I sat down. Then a conversation continued. I can still see my tears dropping into the lentil soup making little circles on its surface. Mary gave me a smile. How could I manage the Latin and maths which utterly confused me? I had missed quite a lot of school during my bouts of asthma, so that can't have helped. Strangely, I do not remember the end of that cheating episode, but some time later, after my Inter. Cert., I gave up both those subjects. Obviously my parents had arranged that with the teachers.

I remember that in second year one of the nuns, judging a project she had given us, said smilingly to me 'You will always be a maverick.' Not knowing whether a maverick was a bad or good thing to be, I didn't tell Daddy until much later.

My own experiences enabled me in adulthood, to empathise with children who had similar difficulties. I hope I was able to be of some help and support to them in coping with feelings of helplessness and fear. At least I was an adult with whom they could share. And, when working in schools, I could liase with parents and teachers where needed.

In my second last school year it was my ambition to become Head of the School when our final year arrived. I was particularly liked by younger children in the senior school and felt a lovely ease with them. I helped them to arrange their games and came in to help at their parties. However, I wasn't particularly good at things academic. I loved English, Art, Religion, was quite good at Irish. I didn't seem to be one of those to whom our Irish teacher said ominously, 'It's no good your wearing out your shoe leather going down to Hume Street.' (Hume Street was the exam centre.) I was moderately good at history and French. I loved drama. There were going to be few if any prizes for me on Prize Day at the end of Fifth Year, the day on which the Head Girl for the following year would be announced. It followed a day when the senior school girls voted, the votes being 'ratified by the Religious'.

The big day came. I think I got two prizes. A few others in my class got nine or ten awards. After that, I must say I greatly admire the staff for not giving an academically clever girl the privilege of being Head Girl. I was given that position which was one of the thrills of my life. Again, that enabled me during my life to encourage children who were not very academically clever to realise that there were other qualities and gifts to develop.

By school-leaving time I had decided that I wanted to have one of three careers: acting, Montessori teaching or journalism. Daddy decided 'Don't put your daughter on the stage'. We didn't argue in those days. At that time the best Montessori training was said to be in London and he didn't want me going over there at seventeen. As for journalism, well, he decided that a year at a commercial college would contribute towards journalism, but also leave me ready to broaden my options. That was how I came to be booked into Miss Dooley's Private School at Haddington Road for type-writing, shorthand, book-keeping and business methods. I wasn't too pleased, but it was just a year of half days plus homework and Miss Dooley was a honey so that was where I started. Some of my shorthand was my own invention and I'm afraid that I kept an eye on the keys of the typewriter. Nevertheless, I got the exams. The next decision did not have to be made. Immediately after the exam results, I was interviewed for a job either in the business office or the medical secretary's office in The National Maternity Hospital, Holles Street, and in the twinkle of an eye I had a job – in the medical secretary's office since my maths had never improved. I was eighteen.

In a short time I was put in charge of distributing and filing the Medical Records in the Out-Patients' Department. Agnes, of course, kept an eye on me. In between clinics I typed, filed and chatted in her bigger office. I loved the job. The women who came to the OPD educated me. Taking it that I was probably fairly streetwise, which, of course, I wasn't, they shared with me little bits about their home dramas, their gynaecological problems and their pregnancies. I kept a dictionary under the counter! Many of the parents brought a troupe of children with them when they attended the clinic. I enjoyed the nursery entailed in keeping an eye on the little ones. Sr O'Brien, the Sister-in-charge of the OPD was a gift both in her sense of humour and her common-sense approach. We became great buddies though she could have been my mother. She gave me the fun I didn't find at home. Home was a serious place.

There is great life in hospital work and we in the offices were not as pressured as hospital staff today. Of course we also had less technology to help us. I loved the opportunities I got of seeing the new-born babies, some so tiny and others 'half reared' when they were born. The Sister looking after them used say of some of them 'Look at him or her! That one's been here before.' My wage was £25 per month – a fortune to me who had £1 per week as a student. Even with that, I gave £5 a month to my mother for my keep. Trust Daddy! He made sure that we undertook such responsibilities. The social life was – as they would say today – mega. I met so many really nice people and we both worked and socialised energetically together. There were hospital parties which led to dates as well as the 'hops' and dances that were lined up outside work. In my spare time I did a bit of writing as I enjoyed it so much and wanted to keep it up. I got a couple of things published.

I suppose all the parties prompted my mother to come out with her next bit of sex education: 'You know, 'she said, 'what married men and women do together?' I told her that I did know. 'Well,' she instructed, 'men want it much more than women do. So wives have to give it to husbands.' I believed that the maternity hospital had taught me more than she realised.

I still dream occasionally about that and about working in Holles Street. I wake up with a sensation of the challenge and buzz I had felt in my job. It was to prove always useful to have keyboard skills, not to mention the insights I gained from the women who came as patients to the Out Patients Department and shared so many of their stories with me as they collected their charts.

6
Whirlwind Years

Sexy? Me? Many people might surmise that because I have written and spoken so often about standards, values and responsibility in sexual life that I must have been asexual. You would be so wrong if you thought that!

From the age of sixteen I was never without a boyfriend. I thought that my boy cousins and their friends were great for a laugh. Then I met, quite casually, the brothers of girls at school or the sons of parents' friends. Boys who were friends rather than 'boyfriends'. I wasn't particularly glamorous or good-looking, but I really enjoyed fun and friendship. I hold, even to this day, that fellows enjoy a girl who has these qualities plus that indefinable whatsit called 'sex appeal'. In my experience you don't have to do anything to be this kind of person. Certainly I didn't. It just happened. My first one-to-one date was on a summer afternoon; back home by 7 p.m. Suddenly I felt my view change though there wasn't the hint of a kiss on those outings. The subsequent hand-holding felt like magic. We progressed slowly savouring all the little delicate advances. And those really were fun years. By seventeen I had joined a tennis club. Sitting around chatting, playing table tennis, meeting the lads and girls. Many a Saturday I danced the early evening away, laughed, talked, flirted. 'Doing what comes naturally' as the song put it. I had to be home by eleven o'clock unless it was a party with a coming-home lift arranged. (Though I came to cancelling the original lift if something more interesting turned up!)

I didn't drink alcohol as I was a member of the Pioneer Total Abstinence Association from the time I was fourteen – and still am. It never spoilt any of the fun. At more formal dances after my 'Debs', I used ask the waiter to make up an exotic fresh fruit juice cocktail complete with green sugar-edged glass and little paper umbrella on top and lots of people wanted a taste. It was called a 'Pussyfoot'. As far as alcohol was concerned, you don't miss what you never had. My partner was free to have what he wanted, but if he was over-indulging, I changed partners. Simple as that. Girls never went to pubs in those days. One day, walking up the mountains with a girl-friend, we came upon an old pub. We decided to peep in and see what it was like. 'What a smell!' was the first reaction of both of us. Then when we came out and ran up the road laughing: it was the row of faces of 'old fellows' up on stools at the wooden counter looking amazed at our intrusion that really finished us with any desire for pub life.

Of course there was no question of sex before marriage and the social sanctions of the day made it much easier for us to avoid that. I honestly think that we had more fun than they have today. An arm around the waist then was a great feeling and I remember having quite a few kisses before I realised that a longer kiss was expected when a friendship was developing. The question of 'What was a sinful kiss?' became a problem for most of us. Was a two-second kiss OK and a five-second one a sin? That was never explained. I always told boyfriends that I had other boyfriends: how could I decide on a partner for life unless I had the experience of a variety of different personalities from which to choose? If they didn't like that they could opt out. My girlfriends and I used to say 'Never run after a man or a bus, there's another along in a minute.' And there was. From time to time we went through a patch where men were 'OUT'. But that always wore off.

On dates we picnicked and walked and snowballed and cycled from Rathgar to Blackrock or Dún Laoghaire swimming baths. I wasn't supposed to go on a boyfriend's motor bike. We went to the zoo, went to a film or play, popped into fancy hotels and had two cups of coffee just to enjoy the atmosphere and watch posh people coming and going. 'Hops' were the discos of that era so I 'hopped' away at the different local tennis clubs on many a Saturday night. With a better-off boyfriend, we had occasional expensive meals. I remember deciding on a mixed grill with one fellow and when he was ordering he asked for 'two mixed grills, one with an egg'. He never even asked me if I'd like an egg! So when the waiter came along with the meals, he asked 'Which of you is the egg for?' and we both said 'Me' together. Another egg was ordered. Fair play.

With another guy I was brought to an expensive restaurant for an Easter outing. I was eighteen and goggle-eyed. I admired the decor and everything that went with luxury. He asked me if I would like oysters. I didn't want to say that I'd never had them. So I said 'Yes'. He said 'How many?' Very floored, I replied 'One would be fine.' He had a great laugh and I asked him how many he was having. When he replied 'A dozen.' I was dumbfounded and suggested that I'd have one of his. My secret was out and I ordered another dish. When I saw the oysters, I didn't even have the one. But that didn't spoil the evening. My dad had a saying 'If you are really a lady you will fit into any situation gracefully.' Maybe that's what he meant, I thought, as I went on to enjoy the date.

At my 'Debs' dance we had a wonderful night. I had the classical white dress, fully approved by my mother. Under it I had a long taffeta waist-slip buttoned at the waist. During one of the whirls on the dance floor, the button opened and down came the slip. I picked it up and, on passing our table, handed it in to one of my girl-friends. That gave us a good laugh. Often after these dances a group of us ended the night on the beach at Malahide having a picnic and welcoming the dawn coming over the sea. We sang, kissed, laughed and paddled. No-one was in the slightest bit drunk, but we really had a ball. My mother wondered how on

earth I got sand on the hem of the evening dress in the Gresham
Hotel. 'How, indeed!' said I, feeling gloriously in love with life.

I made some of my own dresses because I felt that I needed a
change and money was scarce. A few yards of material cost only a
couple of pounds. I 'flew at it' impetuously, and I remember on
one summer date having to wear a cardigan all that warm day
because I'd made a mess of the armholes of the dress. Some of the
lads were penniless students so we kept it simple, others had cars
and were earning, a few had business cars. One taught me to drive
at seventeen, but I didn't think it would be good for my parents to
know that. I never even thought that I might be known as a flirt. I
looked up the word 'flirt' in the dictionary and found that it was
'one who played at courtship; giddy; pert.' So I reckoned that
there was nothing really wrong with that. No-one seemed to get
hurt. We were all the time mixing and matching and I made no
promises. 'I'm not ready yet' I told them. Strangely, if we were out
for an evening at a film, for example, I had to be home by eleven
o'clock and woe betide the fellow who brought me home late. My
father invited him in for a lecture and sent me to my room. But
when we were at a 'dress-dance' until, perhaps, 3 a.m., the parents
seemed to go fast asleep and one could steal in as the milkman
trundled up the road and the sky was pink and azure.

At just twenty I was invited to a party in the home of the son
of a relation. I knew that none of my pals would be there, but as
it was a relation's 'do' my mother encouraged me to go. My
current boyfriend wouldn't be there. I had promised to babysit
that evening from 8 p.m. until 10 p.m. then on to the party.
Towards the end of the babysitting I got into a borrowed dress, put
on the bit of 'face' as we called it and waited. And waited. And
waited. The baby's parents were full of apologies when they
arrived home. By that time I was cross and sleepy. But I was driven
to the party nonetheless. I arrived with the planned explanation
for my lateness. Supper was just over so I drifted rather
desperately into a room where I expected to know few people.
There I spotted an old flame across the room. I wasn't going to

look lost in front of him, so I smiled all around and a fellow near the door asked 'Have you just come?' I told him my situation and he replied 'I'll get you a bit of supper.' He disappeared kitchenwards and brought back a plate piled high with goodies and a mineral. We sat down together in a little comer and shared the spread. Then we danced. I talked brightly so that the 'ex' would see me having a good time. The guy I was with turned out to be really nice, looked handsome and I thought to myself 'My goodness, this is going to add further complications to my love life.' He offered me a lift home and invited me for a date the following Saturday. He was so nice that I accepted. When, eventually we had said a kissless 'good night' I went in home. On arriving in my bedroom, I found that I couldn't remember his name! So, next day, I made up a name for him as I told my mother about the night. After all, I couldn't tell her that I was dating a fellow whose name I didn't know. His name turned out to be Peter Macnamara and we got engaged on my twenty-first birthday. The rest is history.

7
Follow Your Bliss

We married in May, 1953. Our journey to London and thence to Jersey was my first time on a plane. In Jersey we rented a sports car and zipped around the island. The weather was misty for a lot of the time but we were elated and found lots of lovely places, quaint restaurants and danced without curfew. As our honeymoon drew to a close I began to wonder what I would do with my days when Peter had gone back to work. My school friends were either working or still at college. I planned to go further into my old plans of becoming a writer.

We stayed in London for a couple of days on our way home from the Channel Islands. Our stay was in a crummy university residence. I remember it as 'crummy' because I didn't feel too well while we were viewing London. We looked forward to coming home to our little bungalow and really setting up home. I felt quite upset when, on arrival, I discovered that, in an effort to be helpful, my mother had unpacked our gifts and placed the furniture, ornaments and pictures in places of her choice. It wouldn't be easy for me to undo it all and have her disappointed. Better to change things gradually to where we wanted them.

I dropped down to my doctor – Dad – to get something for my upset stomach. He examined me and came up with the verdict. Morning sickness! We grinned broadly at one another. I was pregnant. In the twinkling of an eye I had a big objective.

We prepared the little bedroom for the coming baby whom we had already named by the unisex name of Kim. He or she would have a sunshine room of yellow with floral chintz curtains and little frill around the cot. The cot had been Peter's family cot, which we got from his parents. It needed painting so he got busy on that. My needle and thread flew along the chintz cotton. I must have been like a mother hen, clucking and fussing as I made the nest for my little chick.

At the same time I was teaching myself to cook. My sister, Mary, married a couple of years before me, was much more domesticated. She gave me some recipes, which I tried out on the long-suffering Peter. However, he was from a family of nine children and was consequently very easy to please. I remember he gave me £5 a week housekeeping money. Even then it was tricky to manage on that amount, but it was no way unusual in the fifties. We both liked sausages, rabbit made a delicious casserole and mincemeat could be used in about twenty different ways.

After some months Peter's parents in Co. Limerick agreed to come up to spend a short weekend with us. I got into a flurry of readying for their visit – our first overnight guests. I polished and cleaned even where there was no dust. Got out the new sheets for the spare beds, put vases of flowers around. It all bore great similarity to the 'mummy and daddy' games Mary and I used to play. I reflected later on how useful such imaginative play is for children.

Peter was picking Mum and Dad up at the station while I got the well-planned lunch. There was a joint roasting and crackling in the oven and home-made soup simmered on top when I heard the car arriving. I lifted the saucepan off the hot ring before I bustled to greet them. Guess what? The loop of my oven-glove caught in the handle of the saucepan of soup and the whole thing turned over. The parents came into the hall chatting and laughing. I almost went into premature labour! Out I went to say a breathless greeting leaving the cooker dripping with soup. Of course I had to tell them – their noses were already sensing a burning smell. We all went into the kitchen and viewed the situation. I felt small and far from being the efficient

little daughter-in-law I had hoped to portray. Mum had the presence
of mind to turn off the oven so that the joint would not be a burnt
offering. Then Peter laughed. That broke my tension. We fixed the
parents up in the living-room while Peter and I rescued the
remainder of the lunch. Having a large family. Mum and Dad could
easily turn my catastrophe into a mere hiccough. The rest of the visit
went fine. I no longer tried to impress.

In February 1954 Barbara-Mary was born. A tiny little 5lb 3oz
baby who brought us a giant portion of joy. We were a family.
Exactly a year, less a day, later Geraldine Mary arrived. I had an
immediate sense of their individuality and wondered at how Peter
and I could produce such perfection. Isn't it wonderful how God
sends such an ocean of love with each child? Everyone said it was
good to have two babies close to one another. They would soon be
able to play together. That is, indeed, how it turned out. They came
to call one another 'Bob' and 'Gen' – and still do. I began to keep a
diary of their progress, noting their every burp as well as the ideas
Peter and I had for their upbringing. The £5 housekeeping became
£7. My diary made interesting reading in years to come and started
me on the habit of journalling. I smile when I read a journal entry I
made at the time. It reads: 'Today the Jesuit I went to consult told me
"If you cause your husband to lose seed without having sexual
intercourse, it is a mortal sin."' Sign of the times.

Soon the two babies were sleeping in the guest room and the
little primrose room became the bedroom for Peggy whom Dad
Mac – another doctor – had met in the course of his medical calls and
whose parents were happy to send her up from Limerick to help me.
She was just fourteen and arrived with a bow in her hair, ankle socks
and tee-strap children's sandals; just like a readymade older sister.
There were only nine years between her and me. She was mad about
the babies and a real 'natural' with them giving me a breather when
she proudly wheeled them out in the afternoon. Her wage was ten
shillings a week of which her mother requested she save 7 shillings
and sixpence. Peggy was quite happy with that. She hadn't been used
to pocket money.

Our family had grown so rapidly in a couple of years that we decided to move house. So after a year, bag and baggage were trundled into a fine old house we had found for ourselves in Rathgar. Quite by chance, I was back in familiar territory. It was a lovely spacious home, though not in good decorative repair. We did some patching jobs and planned great refurbishing initiatives which we never had the money to carry out.

By 1957 Clare-Mary had arrived. At birth Clare was a little bigger than her two sisters had been – this time we had a beautiful blue-eyed, curly haired baby who smiled from her earliest days. The older sisters spoilt her outrageously and had to learn that an infant cannot cope with mechanical toys or dolls as big as herself. Soon I had taught them to bring to me any little things they found like screws, elastic bands, keys and so on which became recognised as 'dangerous for little babies'. By then my journalling suggested to me the possibility of my writing some little 'homely thoughts' on being a young mother. Our babies were healthy, thank God, but gave me little time to indulge more lofty journalistic aspirations. I wrote entries such as the following:

> Today Barbara climbed up on their bedroom window-sill. It is broad enough for a child to stand on and we keep the main windows locked. The little latticed fly windows were open and they are operated by loops of cord. Someone downstairs called Barbara. In her play she had put the loop of window cord around her neck. Hearing the call she jumped on to the bed below the window. Thank God the cord around her neck was dried brittle by years of sunshine and it snapped as she fell. I heard her loud cry and found her with a wide graze around her throat from ear to ear. What a horrifying accident that could have been. I explained the danger and together we thanked God for saving her. Parents have to be on the watch all the time.

A few entries in my journal concerned the fact that Clare, at twenty months had not yet walked. She was such a lively little girl and crawled with great speed, dragging one leg. People reassured me but I had a gut feeling that all was not well:

> We brought Clare for X-ray today and she was found to have a fractured leg. I can't remember her having a fall but the doctor told us that it was a green-stick fracture and that she may have twisted her leg in the bars of the cot. Her leg was put into plaster. The other two think that she is cute and are looking after her with great care. She was made their main patient in a game of 'hospitals'. I pray that all will be well.

As, indeed, it was. I've often thought that children prove the truth of the religious concept of 'original sin'. We always have to teach them to be good; they seem to come to come into the world knowing, without teaching, how to be bold. I wrote:

> Today Barbara was deliberately disobedient about the chocolate in the dining-room press. I smacked her. (In those days an appropriate smack didn't seem to do any harm once a hug followed soon after. Nowadays I note children smacking and kicking their parents who don't know how to respond!) Barbara was crying following her smack and Geraldine came running into the room, also crying. 'Why are you crying? I asked her. 'Because I didn't see the smack' she wailed. I hugged the two of them. Mothers are learning all the time.

A couple of years later Uncle John was coming for lunch. During the meal the girls asked him what kind of a job he did. 'I'm an educational psychologist,' John replied. The girls stared at him uncomprehendingly. 'Say a bit of it,' said Geraldine. John always enjoyed that story.

Life for mothers is full of mini-adventures. We had a strong awareness of the fact that babyhood passes quickly. Already Barbara was ready for Infant School. In its deceptive simplicity the rearing of small children is at the core of a healthy society. It matters enormously to a country's well-being that children receive the best formation we can give them at home. The recipe seemed to us to be: plenty of love mixed with discipline, hugging, a sprinkling of giddiness and horse-play, flavoured with security and shared prayer. Presence and availability were key factors.

To express my ideas about family life I wrote a series of monthly articles for the then familiar little red-covered magazine *The Irish Messenger of the Sacred Heart*. The kindly editor, Fr Charlie Scantlebury, SJ, accepted these in 1960 and '61. Little did I know where these were to lead me. My journalistic aspiration kept squeezing out between all the other activities of a young mother. And, of course, being the mother of three, I could also fulfill my love of working with children.

Writing is in my blood. My father, grandfather and uncle did it. I can't remember a time when I didn't do it. But mine was a spontaneous, chatty style, just letting it flow not minding whether or not it gets on the market. Perhaps a surprise letter for someone. Writing has helped me to know who I am and what I truly believe in. I loved when others wrote to me.

In my later teens I had written reviews of children's books. Then in the sixties and seventies booklets and pamphlets. The pamphlets, *How to Choose a Wife* and *Maturing for Christ* cost 6d (old pence) each. I felt that I was getting into the big league with *Living and Loving*, which, in 1969, cost one shilling and sixpence. In 1971 *Happy Families* cost 10p: it started 'Good families can change the world', that's still true, but it is strange how dated the presentation of a book or an article can become.

A lady I'll call Ellen wrote to me from the midlands in 1971. She said, 'I'm married ten years and I never knew about some of the things you said in *Living and Loving*. We have six children and I'm giving them the book when they are old enough to read it. Do you think eighteen would be about the stage to give it to them?' I wrote back saying, 'Get going on telling your older ones these facts of life as soon as you can. Just read a little bit at a time with them during their early years. When they are familiar with the whole book, the great thing is that they will be used to your talking with them about all these matters.'

Ellen wrote back telling me firmly 'The age of eighteen is time enough for them. After all, I've only just learned it myself...'. I felt that a bit longer with TV and chatting with friends would change her.

Parents found this new openness difficult to cope with in talking with their children in a way that no-one had ever spoken to them as they grew up. Gay Byrne on the *Late, Late Show* and radio was contributing much to the changes taking place in Ireland. I appeared as a guest on a number of his TV and radio shows. He was always courteous, forthright and gifted professionally.

8

Creation and Buzz

Though of course I didn't know it, our lovely little Monica was to be the last baby born to us. She arrived in April 1960 to join her three sisters. Barbara was then six, Geraldine five and Clare was three. Subsequently I had three miscarriages. We were unaware that our private little baby-boom was over. I was going to be called into a different area of creativity.

I suppose that, like all mothers of a few children, I was by then a dab hand with babies. In spite of broken nights and the usual sorts of runny noses, and children's illnesses, Peter and I loved children and were very interested in all aspects of their development. I was blessed with Madge, our then home-help, who was great with the children.

In those days many a middle-class mother stayed a full fortnight in hospital or nursing home following the birth of a baby. It was a mini holiday for me. While we were still in the nursing home, the baby was taken out by husband, friends and family to be baptised, as was customary quite soon after birth. I missed the Church ceremony, but I sat up in bed to enjoy the party afterwards! So I was never at the actual baptismal ceremony of any of our children.

I remember the great 'welcome home' we got when at last I emerged with Monica Mary. A couch in the sitting-room was lined with dolls and teddies – all to welcome the new baby and give her an idea of what and who she would be able to play with. A tasty tea was prepared after which the three girls put on a concert for us and for their new sister. It was the first family concert Monica had shared in though, over the years, she not only took part in but also organised many other home dramas. By the end of this first programme Monica was grizzling in the carry-cot. Time for food.

An audience of three stood around 'oohing' and 'aahing' as I fed and bathed their baby sister. Everyone wanted to hold her and to help with the flannel nighties, the nappies and the pins. No such thing as disposable nappies in the Ireland of 1960. All were handwashed daily. There was a nappy bucket in the bathroom in which soiled nappies were steeped awaiting the days washing. I remember sending three-year-old Clare to the bathroom with a nappy to steep. She misunderstood her task and tried to flush it down the toilet with disastrous results. Not unusually, we had not yet been able to afford a washing machine. But we were a post-war generation, used to rations. So what we didn't have didn't worry us too much. However, a second-hand one came our way very shortly afterwards; a stout machine with a hose leading into the sink to remove used water and a detachable mangle into which one fed the wet clothes. No more hand-wringing of heavy, wet clothes. Exit our old mangle. Such a luxury! The daily chore of washing for the family became almost a pleasure.

Looking after my little clutch of children, I decided to write my reflections on being the mother of four under-sevens. The two year series of family articles which were published monthly in the *Irish Messenger* (1960–61) were written by hand (I had no typewriter though I knew how to type). I remember that when the three older children were at the local nursery school, I felt I was free. I scurried to my table in the box-room and did a two hour stint of writing while Monica slept in her pram. I also wrote lengthy letters to the in-laws in Co. Limerick and got great newsy letters from Mum Mac. The mornings are still my best writing time.

I felt I couldn't go far wrong in writing what were my present very real experiences with the children, learned over the past seven years. Peter and I joined some other couples of like age and stage and we spent regular time exchanging experiences and helping one another with ideas and plans for our young families. These meetings were informal precursors of the more formal Parenting Groups of today.

My pen gobbled up the pages. It seems now as though the morning sun always filled that little room and I had found a new source of delight in writing. I always started with a prayer. My mother was the source of my spiritual life – my greatest gift from God through her. What a joy and excitement it was to have these articles accepted. Each month I received the *Irish Messenger* and there was my own name, almost miraculously, in the contents. I still have copies of these articles. They were about love, spoiling, discipline, prayer in the family and day-to-day experiences of humankind. Recently they turned up again and I re-read a few of them. My goodness! How old-fashioned they seemed both in the expression and the presentation of ideas. I had thought that I might show them to my now adult daughters. But they sounded so stilted that I cringed and quietly put them away. Yet they were still 'me'.

The year of the thalidomide catastrophe, when pregnant women were given it to cure their morning-sickness, I read of the tragic outcome of expectant mothers using that drug. I was in the train to Belfast where, as result of the *Messenger* articles, I had been invited to give a talk on marriage and young parenting to student teachers. The butterflies in my stomach as result of the anticipated 'lecture' were silenced by the horror of the thalidomide outcome: babies were being born deformed – some horribly so. I can still remember sitting in that train reading that news. It could so easily have been me.

The only lecture I had given before that was my response to the challenge of my father when I was about nineteen. I had made little of a talk given in the Old Dublin Society (of which Dad was

President) when he commented 'When you are able to give a talk as good as that, you'll be in the position to criticise.' I said that I would do a talk and the title of that, my first public lecture, was 'Master Deighan and his Geography'. Daddy did so much 'checking' of the work that I think of it as mostly his. It is his kind of formal writing. But I did it and presented it to an audience. I enjoyed that; it responded to my liking for being on stage. I imagine that I must have read it word for word; I was too nervous to improvise.

So the Belfast talk was my second time on stage. I enjoyed the buzz of it. It went down so well that it was suggested that I stay on another day and give the talk to the senior school girls. Two successive days of buzz won me over. Two of my ambitions were coming to fruition in unexpected ways: I was on a stage – of sorts – and I was writing. Great! How might I link the two activities? I was paid the princely sum of £5 for my work. Later I bought a tartan skirt and jumper with my earnings.

Home again, I further mulled over the growing-up years as I had experienced them. No great drama there. I was too close to those years of growing-up to think that they might be of interest if written about. There was no such classification as 'teenager' then. It was all merely part of a whole and no particular attention was paid to the moods and independence-seeking of the blossoming young girl or boy. Huffs and answering-back parents weren't tolerated. I might have felt angry, but never expressed it. There was plenty of discipline in our home. Dad laid down the law and there was no discussing his decisions. Mother decided what was proper to wear and told me that I'd ruin my eyesight if I continued to wear my 'silly "Veronica Lake" hair-style.' She had told me little or nothing about my developing body except that it was all good and natural as a girl moved from childhood to being a young woman. Indeed, when at school needle-work 'chat' class I announced that I wanted to be a nurse so that I could find out where babies came from, the nun-teacher phoned my mother and suggested that she tell me a little more. Mum explained the 'Hail

Mary' in some embarrassment: 'Blessed is the fruit of Thy womb'. Hmmm. So that's what it meant. I had never even questioned the meaning of those words.

So now, in the 1960s I got down to a bit of reflection. Girls should know things that I had missed out on in my growing years. I got to remembering my first boyfriend. Since he had been at boarding-school, I had to be satisfied for a long time with a photo of him, which I kept under my pillow plus the earth-shaking – for me – revelation by my cousin that this boy had his eye on me. Remembered feelings, mistakes and experiences seemed to be well worth sharing with teenagers setting out on this voyage of discovery.

So there in 1961 in my little box-room I realised how much there was to share with the present generation of teenagers. I was about ten years ahead of them so I could still identify with what were likely to be their wonderings. There and then I decided to jot down all those points that it might help school-leavers to keep in mind.

It was at that time that Elvis Presley, 'Elvis the Pelvis', was gyrating into our field of vision. Some adults were horrified by this new type of performer. The Beatles were soon to follow. Boys and girls were thrilled with this new sound and clamoured to hear and see all they could of these budding idols. Ireland was being jerked out of its insularity. Across the water 'Flower Power' was becoming evident. We thought at first that the 'Flower Children' were standing for innocence, simplicity and love. We were soon to find out that 'free love' and drugs were part of their hippie-style message. Woops! Ireland was a-changing. I wondered what the school-leavers would be making of these events and thought more and more about sharing with them and getting into their world of thought. Basically I realised that Christian thinking should be firmly based on God's message of love. That needed to be reinforced where tempting new concepts of absolute freedom without responsibility were breaking through.

It occurred to me that I might try to get myself invited into a local school to share my reflections with the seventeen to eighteen-year-old age group and to hear their comments and questions. The idea bubbled excitingly until I finally wrote to a school principal, sharing my idea and sending her a copy of the notes for my proposed 'talk' to her students.

Finally she contacted me and we arranged to meet. After some conversation she accepted my proposal and invited me to her school. Little did she or I realise what a significant move that would prove to be. Many schools were to follow.

****

In 1962 I had my first miscarriage. I was about three months pregnant and had started to haemorrhage. I think I was three days in hospital before the actual miscarriage took place. I was in a cubicle of my own and I realised that the 'mis' had taken place. Using a glass of water from beside my bed, I baptised the tiny piece of what had promised to be my fifth baby. Then I burst into tears. A nurse came in and I was brought to the theatre for the' wash out' that was the D & C. I had been given a light anaesthetic and when I 'came to' the first thing I heard faintly was the cry of a new-born baby. In a daze I thought it was my own and asked the nurse. 'Is it a boy or a girl? Is it OK?' She replied 'You haven't had a baby; that's someone else's child'. In tears again I was brought back to my cubicle. I was ready to go home.

Neither Peter nor I understood the sense of loss after a miscarriage. Clearly a day or two later he thought it was all a matter of the past. I didn't want to appear to be overdoing my feeling of loss, so I, too, tried to be my old self again. I felt drained. I tried to get back and got involved in a bit of writing. At that time I had been writing some little pamphlets.

My second miscarriage went largely unnoticed by anyone else; It was in 1967. I was about seven weeks pregnant and we had gone to the museum with the children and a friend when I felt the bleeding start. I excused myself and went to the ladies' room. Fixed myself up as best I could and continued with the tour of the museum. I told Peter when we got home and decided that an early-to-bed night and a lazy day to follow would be an adequate treatment. So that was, apparently 'it'. I didn't feel too well and was, in fact a bit ashamed of my unshared sadness at a second miscarriage. But I pressed forward with ordinary life. I think that what I wrote after those experiences lacked joy or any sense of fun. I felt serious and depressed.

Finally, I became pregnant again in about January 1968. I had to go to a different obstetrician as my familiar doctor had retired. All was well for, perhaps, two visits. On the third visit the doctor examined me for longer than usual saying nothing as the examination progressed. Then he looked at me and said 'That baby is dead.' It was as stark as that. I was totally silenced. He told me to dress and then I asked him 'What happens next?' He said 'We'll wait until you have a spontaneous miscarriage.' I enquired 'When might that be?' He shrugged 'It may be at any time.' he told me. I asked if I might telephone Peter. So he got his secretary to help me get through to Peter's office. That was it. I was to call the doctor when I saw the usual signs of miscarriage. 'Good afternoon'.

I was dazed. Peter and I went to a hotel for a cup of tea and a chat. It was so nice to be with him. He was always calm and kind. Neither of us knew what to expect next. So we just went home. When I had reached the three months point in the pregnancy, I had told the children that a new baby was due. They had been highly excited. Now I had to tell them otherwise. I remember that after explaining about miscarriage, Monica, then aged seven, put her arm around me and said 'I'm glad you didn't miscarriage [sic] me.' We all hugged each other.

I waited. No sign of the baby being delivered. But at the end of my sister Mary's birthday party in July, three months after my news from the doctor, the miscarriage started. Peter and my brother-in-law notified the doctor and drove me to the hospital. I was haemorrhaging heavily. After a while of waiting in a little hospital theatre, the doctor arrived. He was bright and breezy. 'Nurse', he said 'This is a very brave patient. I think we'll do the D & C without anaesthetic.' He didn't even know whether or not I was brave! I wasn't. It was a horrible experience. For the remainder of the night I was in hospital and in spite of a sleeping pill, I shivered off and on all night. Next day I went home. That was supposed to be it. Margaret, my home help at the time, was due to go off to her family for the coming week. I asked her if she could defer it, but she didn't want to since it was all fixed. I felt really down. Peter was glad 'it was all over.' I felt that it wasn't. But yet I supposed that a couple of days should mend me in body and soul. My work was waiting, everything seemed to be on hold and I realised that I'd better get back to my busy life. There was no real understanding of the aftermath of a miscarriage at that time. I became depressed again.

9

The Time of the Singing Birds

Holidays began at least a fortnight before we set off. Such excitement! We might have been going to any glamorous holiday resort. But we usually went to a guest-house in Kerry or Donegal. I would have looked carefully at the good value available and marked the best and together Peter and I would look at the map and decide. And we were almost always blessed in what we got.

Over the few weeks before the holiday, I tried to put aside the clean clothes, bathing and beach outfits that we hoped we would need. Realistically, I also packed the woollies, the wellies and the raincoats. One can never depend on Irish weather, which calls for a readiness both in clothing and ideas to enable us answer the question, 'What'll we do today?' when the rain shrouded the landscape.

For the first years we had a Volkswagen Beetle. As it aged it got spray-painted in two colours after which the nursery-school goers called it 'Prunes and Custard'. Can you imagine it with two adults in the front, three small children on the back seat like hens on a perch, and, in the space behind the back seat, the carry-cot complete with baby? A luggage rack on the roof made it look ready to take to the air, but the load of baggage placed, jig-saw like, around the children's feet and mine provided a steadying influence and kept us grounded. When we arrived at our destination we almost had to be dug out.

Nothing daunted, we sang along, played car games. One of the children was bound to ask, after about five miles, 'Are we nearly there?' I got to the point of promising a prize at the end of the journey to the one who didn't ask that question. We gave points for 'spotting things' – a church spire, a thatched cottage, a black horse and so on. That made everyone look carefully at the scenery as we drove along. I remember commenting 'Isn't that a lovely view?' Only to be met with the response 'Where?' from one who was gazing out in the same direction as I was. Children take scenery for granted at a young age. All might go well until someone announced 'I think I'm going to be sick'. Everyone jumped to get out of the way. Dad stopped the car. I provided a towel as I rescued the ailing one out from her place on the perch and we all took a stretch and a stroll. Recovery was almost instant. We usually brought a picnic and Peter was masterful in spotting a lovely field or sheltered woodland. If it was private land he used to go up to the farmhouse and never failed to get permission to drive in and have our picnic in the most select spot. One year the farmer's wife joined us and invited the children to see her turkeys. On that brilliant summer's day we booked our turkey for the next Christmas (and a few other Christmas turkeys followed). So Christmas brought lovely summer memories.

The June after Monica was born (in April) we were short of cash, but got great value for our holiday in a little guest-house in Dunkineely, Co. Donegal. It accommodated just one family. The 'bean a'tighe' was delighted to have the baby and to baby-sit when we brought the others to the beach. Baby Monica was bathed in a plastic wash-up bowl. She was a good baby and I remember that it was there that I first heard the phrase 'not a mum'. When we came back from our swims, 'not a mum' meant that the baby had slept solidly. It became a family phrase. A bonfire on St John's Eve was a key event on that holiday. In the dark of the night bonfires were flickering all around the local hills, sparkling like fire-flies. Ours added its flicker to the great enjoyment of the children.

For me it was just heaven to leave Dublin, complete with our little family, and head for the hills and cliffs, the beaches, the waves and the lovely people of somewhere else. We went to places where we could be completely free to wear whatever came to hand and it didn't matter if trousers got stiff from sea-water or tee-shirts green from rolling on grass mounds. Pockets seemed to get full of sand and legs glistened with the brown-gold of the shore. Hand-in-hand we headed into enormous waves where we were thrown around like pebbles. We came up spluttering and laughing and waiting for the next white-capped mountain to engulf us. No one slept less well when the bed was gritty with sand because sun and sea, rock pools and fishing nets and sand castle competitions made sleep come easily. Diving from the pier became another delight as everyone became more proficient at the swimming. It seemed to be worthwhile staying in the water even when fingers turned white and it was hard to get clothes on to sea-sticky bodies. A hug, a helping hand, a boiled sweet and a big towel were great comforts afterwards. On cold days it was delicious to bundle back into 'Prunes-and-Custard' where the thick navy rug covered everyone in the back seat and I took the littlest one inside my Aran cardigan.

In Ballybunion Mrs O'Sullivan was the kingpin. She was an English teacher during term time. When holidays came the brave woman opened her home as a guest house. The house was beautifully situated, overlooking the beach. A winding path with a little stream running alongside it led to the golden sand and the wild ocean. Mrs O'Sullivan was an 'aisy class of woman'. In the middle of preparing dinner for the lot of us she would have the book of Shakespeare sonnets propped up on the dresser to keep her in touch with the finer things as she stirred the gravy or chopped apples for the pie. Her cooking was great: sensible, tasty meals. In those days children ate whatever was put before them – no fads – and they thrived on it. Their question as we came up to dinner was 'Will it be brown meat or chicken?' When the end of the meal came the small lads and girls were banished to the garden so that the adults could chat over their final cuppa. Woe betide any child who drifted back to the dining-room unless there was something very important to report. 'Fix your own rows,' said the mothers. 'O-U-T!' said the dads. The holiday was for everyone. So the children made their own fun while we had an after-lunch chat, snoozed or did the crossword. Then it was all go again.

Mrs O'Sullivan was delighted when our little group of eight children (two families) decided to put on a concert for charity. What a great woman! She entered fully into the occasion, helping to pull together the dining tables to make a stage, rigging up curtains and helping with programme-making. The rehearsing and costume making gave our bedrooms new purpose for a day or two as we readied ourselves. Mrs O'Sullivan's daughter, also a teacher, was an enthusiastic replica of her mother. The evening came and was a wow. The dressing up, make-up and nerves of performers added zest to the occasion and the audience couldn't have been more encouraging. The session concluded with a supper supplied by the home family. A few pounds were sent off to the missions with a letter written by the children describing the event.

On another glorious summer morning during one of our memorable stays in Bunbeg, Co. Donegal with the McGarvey family, I woke up at dawn with the words of a possible poem singing in my head. It began to come alive in my mind. Peter was still asleep and, not wanting to wake him by drawing the curtains, I slipped out of bed, took my paper and pencil, went into the loo where I sat penning the following lines (to be sung to the air of Percy French's 'West Clare Railway'):

Holiday Pleasure

'Ireland of welcomes' they call it,
The welcomes they come big and small
but if 'Céad Míle Fáilte' you're seekin'
Just come to Bunbeg, Donegal.

In a house that they call 'Sruth an nGleanna'
Meet Sarah-Dan, Jimmy and clan
And sure with no scrapin' or bowin'
They'll welcome you in to a man.

The turf fire is ever a glowin',
Food from Sarah-Dan's oven's first rate,
There's always a cup of tea goin',
and the freshest of scones on the plate.

If it's glamour and bright lights you're seekin'
Make your way off to Paris or Cannes,
But if peace and contentment you're needin'
Stop with Jimmy and kind Sarah-Dan.

10

S.W.A.L.K.

When September came I rolled on into other schools just as The Rolling Stones rock group hit the Irish scene. Adults were commenting on the morally destructive influence of The Stones and other emerging pop groups. Young people were sensing something new and exciting in the air. The wind of change rustled restlessly amongst the teenagers. Black and white television was becoming a force to be reckoned with.

Discipline was still strong in the 1960s. When I arrived at the school a teacher or a couple of the girls met and greeted me with due decorum. Accompanied by the hosts I arrived at the classroom. Immediately the girls all stood up and said their 'Good morning' in chorus just as I would have done in school. They didn't sit down until told to do so. (Today there is often chaos). The teacher gave a preliminary introduction and departed. There was total silence. I introduced my subject and a straight talk followed; no teaching aids were expected and no-one interrupted. Usually students stated their preference for writing down their questions during the subsequent break. Neat rectangles of paper were distributed. Then the girls arose, thanked me in chorus and the teacher took over for the break while I was given a dainty cup of coffee in the parlour.

How different all that was to become as the years rolled on.

The questions the girls wrote so neatly (nowadays they scrawl them on any scrap of paper torn from a notebook) were largely to do with a few expected topics: shyness, friendship or lack of it; getting a boyfriend; dating behaviour; what to wear on different kinds of dates; what was or was not sinful in the sphere of kissing; getting on with parents; anticipating marriage and family. In most homes there was firm discipline and little space given for argument or discussion. Life was simpler all around and people had more time. Though exams were always a big deal, they did not cause the excessive anxiety that can often be seen today. The girls' questions from their question box to me were predictable, perhaps because they were so similar to those I and my school friends would have had ten years earlier. The following are examples of the 1960s type of question:

I've an Adam Faith poster in my bedroom. My mother said it's not nice and to take it down. Will I?

Is it a sin to allow long kisses?

What is the best sort of thing to wear on a date to the theatre?

If you have been out with one boy a few times, is it disloyal to date a different one?

What do you think of a girl wearing a bikini?

My father doesn't approve of slacks. What do you think?

I can't talk to my parents about going out with my girl friends and meeting boys. I'm eighteen.

My mother is very old-fashioned. She thinks a girl should be left school before dating.

Is cheek-to-cheek dancing a sin?

I blush any time a boy talks to me. How can I get over that?

Friends say it is right to kiss as a boy leaves you home after an evening. Is it?

What do you do at a hop if no-one asks you up to dance?

How can a couple space their family?

My brothers do nothing to help at home. Is that usual? How can I change that?

My grandmother lives with us. She disagrees with girls going to university. Do you?

As I would not have spoken about sexual intercourse (as per my agreement) there were seldom questions about that. Girls were cagey at first and I didn't want to over-step my mandate – a nice pun there! But gradually, as I became more aware of the sort of questions the girls asked, I also became more confident in talking about periods, pregnancy, and, later, about 'sexual intimacy' (intercourse). By the 1970s The Sex Pistols were loudly proclaiming a new anarchy and the signs of disorder and indiscipline were creeping into the classroom.

Young people rightly wanted to be heard and written questions were being replaced by a still disciplined questioning from the floor. A healthy sign which was becoming reflected at home.

After a year or so I decided to write a series of six articles identifying the areas of interest and concern that were surfacing. I didn't know who might publish these. There was seldom anything written in Irish papers about these topics.

I sent the articles to the *Sunday Press* and kept my fingers crossed. Frank Carty, the genial editor, accepted the articles. They were published in six successive weeks.

The series provoked considerable interest and some questions were sent to me by parents and young people. Frank Carty gave me a couple of additional weeks to respond to these questions. What was published underwent careful scrutiny; there were certain no-go areas.

The 'few weeks' turned into about twenty years! I became an 'Agony Aunt' without ever having planned to do so. I would never have thought of setting myself up in that role. It just happened. As I got to know the real pain behind people's letters, I objected to the derisive term 'Agony Aunt', but people applied it automatically. My husband, Peter, was always honest and encouraging about 'the column' as it came to be known at home. He was great when questions about boys and men came up. The children didn't pay much attention to it at first, little knowing that it would last through their teen years and cause them some moments of embarrassment and teasing. Being 'Angela's daughter' wasn't going to be an easy role. I was known for taking a moral line and 'no messing'. I also advocate prayer as a wonderful source of support in troubled times. Not the approach that everyone wanted to hear in the changing Ireland of the sixties.

It was too late then for me to write under a pen-name, but I always wished I had done so from the start. Nevertheless, our girls managed to have plenty of fun and they survived the slagging.

Our own parents and adult siblings showed a measure of disfavour for my position. My father took a poor view of the form my journalistic ambitions had taken. I was a source of embarrassment. My quiet and gentle father-in-law gave his approval and encouragement. I remember one family member introducing me to friends and adding ruefully 'Yes, that's who she is.' At social events there was a lot of joking, with people expressing 'My wife needs you. Ha, ha!' and such like. Soon I became recognised on the street – following being on the *Teen Talk* TV programme with Bunny Carr, and having my photo in the paper each week. As I flew around the supermarket, I was often nabbed by someone who wanted to bring me behind the packets

of Cornflakes for a little 'sharing'. Not Cornflakes! I had to learn
how to avoid that sort of session. But the general public were
usually very kind and accepting.

Many people wrote to me in the *Sunday Press*. Over half of
them sent stamped envelopes hoping for a private reply. The editor
wanted only three or four letters for the column. He made it clear
that if I responded privately to others it was my choice and
responsibility. But I couldn't read them and just put them in the
waste-paper bin – along with their stamped envelopes. There was
loneliness, hurt, depression, anxiety, abuse of different kinds
including all the ills of alcohol abuse. Rejection, fear and remorse
– indeed all human pain was represented there. Seduced by the
very real agony of people, I found myself answering more letters
privately than for the column. At first I was paid, I think, £15 per
week for the column and that mounted to about £25 per week
towards the end of my twenty years 'tenure of office'.

I began to realise how therapeutic the writing of the letter had
been for the troubled person. Again and again letters were
concluded with 'Thank you for listening', or 'It has been so helpful
to write all this to you.' They felt that I was a friend who would
not reveal their sufferings. Letter-writing took on a new depth of
meaning for me, which I hoped to translate into a letter-
counselling service later on.

People often asked me if I made up the letters. But I had far too
many genuine letters to have to do that. They thought that people
were having me on. But I reckoned that any question that was a
fairly regular question would be interesting to publish whether or
not it might be a joke. Some were very obviously joking with old
chestnuts such as 'I'm getting tired of my boyfriend. He has a
wooden leg. Do you think I should break it off?' We got a good
laugh from some of the joking letters. I shared non-confidential
letters at home and over our evening meal we often discussed the
possible reply. My daughters didn't always agree with me. I began
to experience, first hand, the changing face of Irish youth. I didn't
learn easily how to give up my expectations of pleasant affability

all the time. Teenagers were beginning to insist on being seen and heard. Our own family experiences were a great help in my understanding of other families.

From my post-box I got plenty to smile at in a sort of warm way. One very elderly lady wrote to me enclosing a ten-shilling note and asking me to send her 'A relic of The Sacred Heart and one of Our Lady too'. I replied returning her ten bob and explaining why her wish couldn't be granted. I sent her a prayer leaflet instead!

Then there was the housewife who sent me a piece of material about the size of a stamp and a cheque for £20 asking me if I could get her four yards of the material in a named Dublin shop. She told me, magnanimously, that I could keep the change. I had a friend working close by that shop. So we managed to get the curtain material at a little extra cost, delighted that it was still available. My friend posted it off to the country. The woman acknowledged the parcel with a note to say 'It's a little pinker than the original.' Her original curtains had probably faded, but I wasn't about to take on that problem.

'Bill' (not his real name) was quite a typical bachelor. He was about forty-eight and keen to get a wife. In a letter of over twenty pages which smelt of tobacco, he described himself, his house, his mother who lived with him, his dog and the job he hoped to get. I particularity remember his saying 'I'm not fussy and a few cobwebs don't worry Mammy.' The girl he had in mind should be about twenty-one. I had no-one suitable in stock, but sent him the leaflet about The Knock Marriage Bureau and other marriage introduction agencies active at the time, plus a few little tips about his stated requirements. He had sent me an SAE and a photo of himself with his bike (photo to be returned). Occasionally a man wrote to me suggesting that I myself might be a suitable spouse if not otherwise engaged! That was flattering. I was considered to be flirtatious, but I had to be careful not to give the wrong ideas to the 'Bills' of this world!

Widowed Liam wrote to me. Tragically he was left with six young children to rear on his own. Such a courageous man, but he needed help. He asked me various questions. An elderly aunt and uncle came to live with the family. After a couple of years and as a youngish man he really wanted a new wife, but didn't know where or how to find one. Together we took on the search. It took a few years, but with perseverance a lovely and eligible woman turned up. We are still in touch and those children have turned into successful young adults. I rejoiced in that story of answered prayer.

'Angela Macnamara, Dublin' became a sufficient address by which to find me. On the back of the envelope many people wrote S.A.G. (St Anthony Guide). Some clever St Anthony lookalike in the post office did the guiding of such letters. S.W.A.L.K. (Sealed With A Loving Kiss) was another decorative – or daring – addition to the back of envelopes. Not knowing what to expect next made my job so interesting. But there was much more to be done in streamlining the whole business. My spare bedroom was bursting at the seams with files and a growing share of second-hand equipment begged, borrowed, but not stolen!

I so wanted to share the need for education in human relationships that I contacted the then Minister for Education, Mr Donagh O'Malley. He invited me to meet him and we had a most interesting conversation. A further meeting was arranged. Tragically, before that meeting took place, Mr O'Malley died. He was a great loss to the country and was sorely missed.

11

Women and Boys

In the 1960s and 70s the sexual revolution had taken off. Headlines boomed about 'Women's Lib.', 'Feminism' and 'Women's Rights'. Women got up on their horses and galloped off in all directions, heady with expectations, but without clear and calm guidance or forethought. Equal pay for equal work seemed to be fair, as did the idea of men sharing equally in the responsibilities of the home. At last women would have control of their own lives, whether single or married. This all suggested the right of a woman to continue in her job after marriage and to use contraception. The notion of sexual liberation seemed exciting, but got disconnected from concepts of reality and responsibility. Strident women began to create their own angry and man-hating agenda. Many men felt very threatened in their role.

Questions put to me in different ways included: 'What would happen if single girls and women agreed to contraception? Where would that end up?', 'What would happen to children if mother was as much away from home as father?', 'Should women abdicate their mothering responsibilities?', 'Why shouldn't we do our own thing?' The way forward seemed to call for compromise and recognition of the fact that neither sex was ever going to be completely free. Children have rights too. But all this had to be learned, often through hard experience.

In the summer of 1968 came the pronouncement from the Vatican on contraception. *Humanae Vitae* was the document that

reiterated the fact that 'Human Life is Sacred' and that there was
to be no artificial contraception for Catholic women. I remember
exactly where I was when this news emerged. We were on
holidays in Donegal. In modern parlance, we were 'gob-smacked'.

At first I read whatever was published in daily newspapers and
Catholic weeklies. It affected me as it affected the majority of
other people. I was a mother in my thirties and had four children.
People had been sure that responsible contraception would be
permitted to married couples. We were going to have to discover
new approaches. The Encyclical has beautiful passages on ideal
married love, which need to be read and reflected on, but not all
marriage partners could claim constant idealism. Quite simply, for
married people to relax together in bed, seldom making love to its
natural conclusion, seemed to be pie-in-the-sky. Many people
never got down to reading the full text of the document. Yet, if
contraceptives were brought in at all, abuse seemed inevitable.

In the early weeks I did not receive many letters on the subject.
But then the volume began to grow. There were women with
selfish husbands; women whose own needs for intimacy were
great; couples who had very little other pleasure in life; men
whose demands of their wives after excessive alcohol were
unreasonable; couples who argued and fought about the meaning
of the Encyclical; people who were drained by the demands of life
and sought solace in intimacy with one another. I contacted a few
priests for advice as to how to deal with all such questions from a
compassionate but moral viewpoint. I received a variety of
responses from the tough line, the ultra conservative, to the line
that said 'encourage them to do their best'. At first my responses
swung somewhere in between. Suggesting that couples speak to
their own priest in the privacy of the confessional, brought me to
realise that 'shopping around' for an understanding priest had
begun. There was an unseemly, but understandable, rush for the
'easy man'. Even from the early stage, the public were not taking
this Encyclical 'lying down' (if I may pun on it). A lot of soul-
searching went on. Many people were strongly tempted to disobey

the Church teaching, felt that too little consultation had taken place that included ordinary married people and argued that 'the Church has no place in people's bedrooms.' We did not then anticipate future problems when teenagers were to protest their right to contraception and exploitation was to become commonplace. Many teenagers were to become emotionally confused and vulnerable. But that was not obvious until later.

Some people argued that it was a women's problem. Others recognised it as a shared challenge that could bring husbands and wives to a deeper level of communication, prayer and love. As an ideal adopted by one partner and rejected by the other, it could wreck relationships. There was a significant link between the subject of the Encyclical and the hue and cry regarding women's liberation.

Since I worked at my writing at home and gave my schools' sessions mainly during school hours, and since Peter was helpful at home, we didn't feel any need to change our mutually agreed arrangements about work. We also had home help. In the matter of sexual fertility, natural family planning was the way we wanted to explore. There was little information to begin with. I certainly felt able to identify with couples who had all sorts of problems to contend with in this sphere.

By 1970 schoolgirls were beginning to ask questions about family planning and women's rights. Society was becoming more secular and women were recognising that they had every right to be more expressive of their needs – social and sexual. That wasn't immediately recognised. I spoke of the need for equality, but not sameness. Each sex has unique gifts and the need was that each learn to express their gifts for their own development and for the equal rights of one another. While women were no longer going to be seen as powerless and inferior I had hopes that they would not lose their gifts for caring and mothering. It was to become hard for men to experience their age-old freedoms being eroded. Adjustments would take time and both sexes would be called to goodwill and patience. Little did we consider the possibility of 'Children's Rights' turning into 'children's autonomy.'

At that time women's magazines were beginning to promote casual sex. The only 'value' seemed to be to use contraception. Adultery, not to speak of fornication, became bad words. We needed to come face to face with these subjects. This was reflected in the questions asked in the classrooms in the 1970s. In a healthy way, a few braver souls were beginning to ask questions from the floor (as well as continuing with the Question Box). Many people, then and since, ridiculed me for advising against pre-marital sexual intercourse and writing of it then as, objectively 'corrupt and sinful'. The opposite seemed to me to turn a blind eye to what could become, in many cases, exploitation and 'sex for kicks'. For Christians and for those of other religions who respect the Bible, God had spoken clearly on this subject. While a new freedom was welcome, it needed to be subject to the teachings of the Higher Power. At that time the destructive philosophy of 'individualism' had not yet taken hold. We had to wait and see.

By 1980 I was receiving invitations to speak to younger age-groups during the school day and to their parents on an evening beforehand. The parents were very supportive and I shared with them the importance of my initiative in school being picked up at home. It matters so much that parents talk with their children on these topics. I had written a booklet to help the parents in sharing with their children at home. The vast majority of parents attending these meetings were mothers. Fathers were (and are) not yet prepared to take an equal share in this responsibility for their sons and daughters. In the schools I began to allocate time to private 'chat' sessions to any girl who wanted to talk to me about a confidential matter. I was amazed at the number who made that choice and at their telling me that they found it extremely difficult to bring up intimate subjects for discussion with their mothers. An additional difficulty became that of there being 'no time' for personal discussions with Mum; sports, ballet, swimming, drama, extra classes, had mothers driving around like whirling dervishes. But no time for relaxed chat. Home had become a busy and often stressed place.

Enter boys' schools! They too were looking for a similar service. I didn't know if I could respond to it. But I'd only find that out if I tried. Boys were different. I knew how difficult young men would find it to talk about sexuality, relationships, morality and their own difficulties in these spheres. I found teenage boys shy, awkward and self-conscious. They were much more concerned than girls about their image in front of their peers. They did not want to indicate any ignorance so they avoided questioning. I reverted to written questions and they asked only a few – some joking ones to which they signed the names of other lads. I never read the names aloud anyway so they were disappointed to miss the anticipated craic. The very few who used the private sessions came in a furtive way, hoping not to be seen by their peers. Some of them had very real problems and, after we had spoken, they liked me to make sure that the corridor was clear before they made their getaway! I knew that they needed help, but reckoned that a male counsellor in an ongoing position in the school could be especially helpful to boys. Girls would also gain from ongoing help, but in those years the idea of having a 'resident' counsellor was not on the agenda. Working with boys certainly helped me to understand how different boys were compared to girls of similar age or even younger.

In the 1980s I was invited to speak with boys in sixth class (primary school). It was a baptism of fire for me. They giggled and punched and laughed – while at the same time not wanting to miss any juicy information I might be ready to share. Serious boys had little hope of learning much as they were shouted down by fellows who wanted to be heard asking vulgar questions in the crudest language. This drew the cheers of their mates, which bolstered their desired self-image as 'hard men'. I remember one lad having his hand up for clarification of a matter that was bothering him: 'Miss,' he asked, 'You had four children, so I suppose that means you done it four times?' (Cheers). I wondered how many had got it right. Fortunately one brave soul opted to put Johnny right, which he did amid further cheers. I got 'runs' of attention when I suggested that they choose whether to allow me talk or decide to talk to one another all the time. They chose me – for short patches of time. I sent one ringleader to the Principal. He returned in about ten minutes looking very contrite. He said that he had been told to apologise and ask to be taken back. I gave him a chair right under my nose. Later I discovered that he had never gone near the Principal! Role-playing with the lads proved to be a greater drama than I had anticipated. Those who volunteered for the acting were the extroverts, and they added drama such as jumping with blood-curdling yells from tables. Their understanding of peer pressure meant physical pressure, to the huge amusement of the audience. I had to call a halt for some more explanatory input. Whew!

One day a twelve-year old lad sitting right in front of me rather ostentatiously produced a condom. At first I pretended not to notice, but as he stretched and snapped it the lads around him found it impossible to control their snorts of laughter and signs of approval. Others became curious. I said quietly, 'Séan, I see you have a condom there. Perhaps you'd lend it to me so that I'll be able to talk about condoms later on.' I put out my hand for the condom, which he meekly handed over. Hardly looking at it, I went on with what we had been saying. Later I was able to get comparative peace when I said 'If you go on messing, we'll have no time to talk about condoms.' 'Shhh' they shouted at one another.

In a mixed school I worked for a day with a group of sixth-class girls. I was due to meet the boys in that school the next day. 'Don't tell the boys all we've talked about. They'll learn tomorrow,' I told the girls. Then, after midday break in the yard, two little girls came bursting in to me, 'Amy and Elsie told the boys!' they announced. 'What did they tell them?' I asked, picturing the scene. 'They said "We know all about youse now"'. I felt that wouldn't spoil the plot!

Gradually I decided to leave the boys to the men who would have better understanding of them. But very few men emerged who felt able for this work. People asked me if I ever took mixed classes: I had tried and found that it didn't work. Young adolescents needed to learn the basics of sexuality within a group of their own sex. At a later age they could be brought together. It is interesting to have them discuss these subjects together and debate their expectations of one another. There would still be innuendoes, double meanings and laughs, but these were also more subtle sources of learning about one another.

12

If the Shoe Fits...

One evening I was due out to a convent on the north side of the city where, in the adjoining hall, I was to give an important talk. A bishop was presiding. All day I had butterflies in my stomach. Legions of them. Yet the doings of the day at home had to be looked after.

My best suit was laid out on my bed with a crisp white blouse, the tights and the high-heeled shoes. The notes were on the kitchen counter where, every so often, I had a peep, used a highlighter, and tried to reassure myself that I was well-used to thinking those written thoughts. I was at risk of high-lighting the whole thing since I thought that it was all important.

Our evening meal was finished when I began readying myself. To look as well as possible was an important boost to my confidence. A final prayer and at last I was on the road, complete with the butterflies. I always had – and still have – difficulty with finding unfamiliar venues. But Peter had briefed me well.

I arrived, unsure of which of all the doors in the huge building was the one at which I was expected to launch myself. The decision shakily made, I parked.

Just as I was getting out of the car, I looked down. Horror of horrors! On my feet were my comfortable old slippers! I had forgotten that last minute habit of stepping out of my comfort zone and into the 'high heelers'. How could I go on stage? What

little confidence I had built up drained out of the soles of my feet.
I sat down in the driver's seat to think. There was no time to go
home. So up I went to the convent door. I tried to explain to the
elderly and deaf Sister who I was, and had only to point to my feet
to indicate my problem. I asked her if any Sister could lend me a
pair of size six shoes for the evening. With a twinkle of
amusement in her eye she fluttered off into the depths of the
convent. I sat down on the carved oak seat in the hall and decided
against looking at my watch or my feet. A great moment for
meditation!

Along came the Sister with a broad smile and brandishing a
large looking pair of black, shiny, laced shoes. My mother would
have called them 'sensible' shoes. I could have hugged the Sister. I
tried on the shoes. Whatever about the style, they fitted. Sister was
thoroughly enjoying this high point of her evening. My evening
was due to start in a matter of minutes. I almost ran, arriving at
the hall somewhat breathless. Through a side door I glimpsed the
desk from which I would be giving the talk. On it was draped a
velour table-cloth which hung to the floor and would hide my feet.
Prayer is always heard in the end, but one can wonder at the
quirky sense of humour of the Holy Spirit. There were no nudges
amongst the audience. It all went according to plan and I forgot
about my feet.

Many and varied invitations dropped through my letter-box.
They came from all over the country. Sometimes I stayed in the
convent, other times I was put up in a B&B, and on very special
occasions in a comfortable hotel. My talks extended to youth clubs
and ladies' groups. The away-from-home schools' talks usually
entailed working with the parents at night and with the children in
the local school next day – maybe for two school days. It often
depended on the number of 'streams' in a particular class group.

One invitation came from Co. Wexford. I was invited to speak
at an Adult Education conference. The host was Fr Séan Fortune
(of subsequent ill repute). I was to stay overnight at the parochial
house. I went by train and was met by Fr Séan, a larger-than-life

man with a blustering, loud and forceful personality. His house
was unexpected. It, too, was large with some valuable paintings
and artefacts. I realised that he took inordinate pleasure in his
possessions. He talked to me about how he came by some of
these. I felt him to be a boastful man, full of his own importance.
But I also realised that some people are like this to compensate for
something that is awry or missing in their lives. I felt that Fr Séan
was big and loud only on the outside. Maybe there was a hurt child
inside. We were joined for tea by a couple of committee people
and Fr Séan was a very enthusiastic host. After that we went to the
venue for the talk. All must have gone well because I don't
remember anything of that particular session.

Later, knowing that Séan Fortune was connected with the
Communications Institute, I shared with him my idea of making
an audio cassette of imaginative stories of the fifteen mysteries of
the rosary. I thought that the stories might help families to share
in prayer and might refresh for other people their approach to the
familiar decades. At the end of each of the stories there is one Our
Father, one Hail Mary and one Gloria. People who wanted to say
the full ten Hail Marys could switch on and off their cassette
player to do so. Fr Séan seemed to be immediately interested and
we arranged to meet at the Communications Institute where, I
understood he had no difficulty in getting recording facilities.

This plan went ahead. Again Fr Séan seemed larger than life
and in his element doing the recording. He didn't strike me as
having much insight or sensitivity into what I was trying to do, but
was well acquainted with his role. At one stage he got some
Lourdes hymns added between the stories, but these were of poor
quality and he agreed to my alternative plan.

Eventually, the cassette was made and he wanted me to spread
around some posters advertising it and to speak of it through the
paper and the other spheres of influence I had. He would do
likewise. I'm not very good at that end of things, but we made
quite good sales. It paid its way, but neither Séan nor I was set to
make any money out of the project. I received some very kind

letters about the production over the coming months. At another time Seán asked me to contribute to his 'Dial-a-Meditation' telephone initiative – which I did. He was full of inventive ideas.

That was the end of my contact with Fr Séan Fortune whose name was to become so well known in the tragic saga of child-abuse in the years ahead. I reiterate: maybe there was a hurt child inside. What a legacy of pain he left behind. We never know the depth of pain some people are carrying. Child abuse must never be tolerated. Radical changes need to be made in Church structures to facilitate openness and acountability.

Letters were still coming in from the *Sunday Press*. Every morning I felt a sense of 'What will today bring?' I enjoyed the buzz and the challenge, but was saddened by the number of people whose letters went unanswered. One morning amongst the rest of the letters was a poor-quality envelope with what looked like a very fat letter inside it. When I opened it out poured over £700 in all denominations of notes. This was accompanied by an anonymous note asking me to pay this conscience money to a given name and address and to acknowledge its payment in my *Sunday Press* column under a given nom-de-plume. At that time I had been dealing with different amounts of monies sent to me for charities and as conscience money and subsequently acknowledged by me in the *Press*. I lodged all these monies in my account and paid for them by cheque requesting receipts for clients who might like to know that I had these. This became big business and I dealt with thousands of pounds, but never again a sum so great in cash as that £700.

I also received hate letters and pornographic letters, samples of pornographic materials available. These were almost always anonymous and simply went into the waste-paper bin carefully shredded. But I did pray for those who had sent such mail. They must have been sick to do so. There were also letters of disagreement with something I had published and these had proportionate chance of publication or private response. I learned from some of the wise suggestions made in disagreements. So I was always learning in one way or another.

In 1978 I became increasingly aware of the need for trained personnel to speak on 'Education in Human Relationships' in schools and clubs. I had ten times the number of invitations any one person could undertake. So I made a suggestion to the committee of the Catholic Communications Institute of Ireland (CCII) that I might address them on this need. I planned to make a presentation illustrating the different aspects of this work as I was experiencing it. I hoped that CCII might be willing to set up courses for potential workers in this field. I felt that if the Church did not do so the work would soon be undertaken by secular groups who had little or no interest in the spiritual or moral aspects underlying the work as I conceived it.

A date was agreed for my presentation. The audience would consist of about twenty-five committee members, all influential people. I was helped enormously by a social worker friend of mine who did some research on programmes of this kind available in other countries. So along came what was another very significant night for me. Along with my friend we presented our findings under different headings. We were as frank and forthright as we could be in outlining the position: Ireland was growing up, new influences were apparent; children were, in turn, confused and excited by the new 'freedom' that was being sold to them. Freedom without responsibility. Parents were perplexed sensing the challenges to their own authority, wanting to go forward, but not knowing how to deal with this new 'breed' of youngster. Discipline was slipping. The moral authority of the Church was being questioned. It seemed to me that the Church had to take new initiatives, make major changes in trying to understand and listen to people and respond with enlightened and modern communications programmes. It was a call to move on, face reality and influence it positively and imaginatively. There was no time for dawdling.

The presentation seemed to be received with interest. Perhaps it was thought to be naïve, but nobody said that. Someone spoke vaguely of the difficulties in such a project. I was told that the whole matter would be considered and that we would be informed about the outcome. I heard no more. Nothing seemed to happen. Neither children nor parents were receiving help in the area of Human Relationships and Sexuality. I was receiving more invitations and more questions to be answered either through the *Sunday Press* or privately. It seemed to me that an important opportunity for change had been missed. I still think that there was an exciting chance there in the 1970s to 'get with' our changing society and show the Church as a living, listening, modernising force in Ireland. The seas were becoming rougher: we needed ballast on the ship.

13

'Please, Bishop, Help!'

While out at a school during the day I was usually home by the time my own clan returned from school. Sometimes my head was whirling. I nipped up to my bedroom and took sixty, not forty, winks. Then I caught up with the children's school doings and the housework. On those days I didn't return to my desk at home until after the evening meal. I began each work session with a prayer, sometimes a half hour's meditation cleared my brain wonderfully. I often worked on letters then until after midnight some *Sunday Press* copy, some private letters. Sadly, at that time I neglected to keep in touch with old friends, I just kept promising them and myself that I would do so ... after this. That is always a mistake.

I made other friends in the course of my work. I was blessed with a young nun-typist, Sister S, who offered her expert help in the evenings. She worked in the spare room on an ancient typewriter and got a wonderful amount of work done for me. She was a whiz with the tape recorder even though it was a reel-to-reel model. Peter, with his engineering expertise, was something of a 'Heath Robinson': updating ancient equipment. In order that Sister would not have to use the manual 'pause' button, he bored a hole in the button, attached a long length of string which had, on the other end, a loop into which Sister could slip her foot. Voila! Pause facility afoot! She and I used be absolutely exhausted by the time we reached midnight. Sometimes we were both giggly with exhaustion. But she made a world of difference to me. We used discuss some of the cases we dealt with and try to work out what might be best to do for the client. A few years later the *Sunday Press* provided me with recording equipment that worked well for us.

I remember Sister S and I looking at a pathetic little letter from 'Rosie'. It went something like this:

> I am fifteen. I am fat and plain and lonely. No one wants to be my friend. I love animals better than people ...

Poor little Rosie! Sister S and I had discussed Dale Carnegie's book *How to Win Friends and Influence People*. It was a book often joked about, but it had nuggets of real wisdom, which I used when trying to encourage friendless people. I suggested to Rosie that she offer her help at weekends to either a local pet shop (named) or to a nearby stables. She let me know some weeks later that she had a Saturday afternoon job in the pet shop and loved it. That was in about 1968 or '70. Imagine my amazement when, about ten years later, Rosie wrote to me and told me that she now owned the pet shop she had helped in as a schoolgirl. She was married and they had a baby girl. She was full of joy. So, great things happen for Agony Aunts (a title I resented since it ignored the very real agony of the correspondents and the effort of the counsellor in responding to them. I learned to hack it.)

That reminds me to tell you about Margaret. She was about twenty when she wrote in desperation saying that her life was going nowhere and that she was utterly depressed. Margaret had had a childhood illness that resulted in her being just over four feet tall. At dances or clubs the boys paid no attention to her. Girls didn't pal with her. People stared unkindly, and looked away. Could I help?

By then I was assembling what I called my 'Helpers List'. It listed all the people throughout the country who had offered their professional help or caring to any of my clients who lived in their area. There were two people working in Margaret's area. So I asked one to find out the whereabouts of Margaret's home. I went down in the train and he drove me to meet Margaret. After a long talk I took the next step of introducing her to Fr M who was in touch with all the youth activities in the area. What a devoted priest he was. He helped her to get to a typing class, which went well. Margaret was a bright girl. He kept regularly in touch with her. The three of us prayed. By that time I had a lengthy list of people for whom I tried to remember regular prayer. The good Lord knew about them all – and about me – anyway.

Don't anyone tell me that miracles don't happen. From London I got a letter from a lonely young man, James, who was also friendless and feeling hopeless because of his very small stature. Yes! You've guessed. With the permission of both James and Margaret I put them in touch with one another. They corresponded, met and, about a year later, they married and settled down in Ireland. They now have a son in his twenties and have a happy and busy life. James is in the writing world and Margaret is a secretary and typist. Their lad is a student. They contact me every Christmas (like a number of others). Stories like theirs have made it all so worthwhile for me. Of course there were also those from whom I never heard again until, maybe, they hit another bad patch.

The letter 'mountain' grew to a point where there was no catching up with it. I became more and more concerned about all the letters that remained unanswered. Some were anonymous and there was little hope for them when the column each week accepted only three or four letters. I felt that more helping agencies should be available in each diocese. So I wrote to the then Archbishop of Dublin, Dr John Charles McQuaid, seeking an interview. I subsequently received a note inviting me to come to Archbishop's House.

We had only one car at that time and I was not scheduled to have it on that day. So off I set across the city by bus. When I arrived I was brought into a parlour to wait. It was one of those brown rooms smelling of beeswax with a huge mahogany table and gloomy pictures on the walls – probably of saints, popes or bishops. It was oppressive and I felt anxious.

In a short time a rotund and formidable nun swept into the room. She introduced herself. Almost straight away she advised me to give up both my schools' work and the *Sunday Press* column. She found them 'distasteful'. This was a bombshell. I refused to agree to her request and said that I would have to make enquiries and get a consensus of opinion from others. I explained what I valued in the work. But 'the lady was not for turning'. She told me that if I didn't give up the work she would advise the schools of her Order to cease inviting me. Then she stood up angrily and I thought she was going to bring me into the Archbishop. Instead she led me to the hall-door and opened it. I didn't even get a look at the Archbishop. But I was to try again – and succeed on the second attempt.

The next time I made that journey was in February, 1967. It poured as I struggled against a gale up the avenue to what used be called 'The Palace'. A strong wind like that was a fairly sure way to bring on an attack of asthma. And it did! This time there was no sign of the nun. Neither did I have time to regain my breath. I was brought, wheezing, into the Archbishop's room. A huge room in which the desk alone was nearly the size of my box-room. (Might not an unpretentious, dignified and comfortable room be more suitable for certain interviews?) I suddenly felt small, anxious and unsure. I had written to the Archbishop so he had an idea of what I was going to say. He was gracious, but cold. So, given my asthma and the anxiety, I burst into tears. Well, he looked utterly taken aback seeming not to know what one does with a weeping woman. The coldness went from his demeanour, and he made some gentle comment. I pulled myself together and told him my worries about all the

troubled people having no-one to turn to. I felt that to have
centres for letter-counselling as well as person-to-person
counselling in each diocese was a Christian responsibility. I asked
him what else I could do. He told me that I was doing my best
and that he would look into the matter. He arose and went over
to the vast bookshelf where he picked out a book and
autographed it for me. It was entitled *Pére Lamy* by Comte Paul
Biver. I shall never know why that was the book he chose. He said
kindly 'Goodbye' and, breathing a bit more freely, I faced the long
avenue in the other direction feeling a mixture of satisfaction and
mortification. What a show I'd put on! In later years I was
warmly welcomed by Archbishops Ryan and Connell. They
contributed an annual cheque to help my work, as did all the
subsequent Archbishops of the Dublin Diocese.

Shortly after that The Catholic Marriage Advisory Council
(now Accord) gave its first training course for counsellors in
Dublin. I attended the selection conference and later, having been
accepted for the year's course, began my studies. I was so glad,
even at that late stage, to have that basic qualification in
counselling. I continued my usual work during the time of the
course; it was a bit like putting the cart before the horse. Later I
was to do some summer holiday counselling courses and a
communications course with Bunny Carr and Barry Baker, which
I thoroughly enjoyed. I was beginning to feel a sense of being
equipped properly for the job. I was writing some little pamphlets
and had become involved with the 'Problem Page' in *Woman's
Way* magazine in its early days. With changing times and
changing editors this initiative drew to a close

14

R. S. V. P.

'The pitfalls of teenage dating' was the title of a section of one of my 1963 *Sunday Press* articles. It suggests a union of ideals that would have a great struggle for expression in a Sunday newspaper today: purity, prayer, prudery and popularity – the Four 'P's. I wrote:

> A sense of humour is vital in protecting one's purity. Prayer is also vital. A prude can do little good simply because she won't be dated. The smart, popular girl, who is good fun, can do great work to encourage the virtue of purity. Boys must learn respect for girls and realise that when the time comes for them to choose a wife, they will want a girl fresh and pure, not a shop-soiled one … I cannot understand the irresponsibility of parents who allow, even encourage, their teenage sons and daughters to emigrate, without having told them anything of the potential dangers they will meet. Many of these young people going abroad have never heard of birth control and the word 'contraception' is foreign to them. They are introduced to these evils under the guise of 'the modern way of living'. Certainly indiscriminate love-making is modern and sex perversions common, but why leave our children dangerously ignorant and bless what we call their 'innocence' as we ship them abroad … Fr Satler's

book *Parents, Children and the Facts of Life* gives most
excellent suggestions to parents as to how to deal with
almost all the situations that may normally crop up.
Sunday Press 31 March, 1963

Forty years ago Ireland was emerging from the veil of secrecy and
silence which had surrounded the subjects of human sexuality and
understanding oneself. On 14 April 1963 I wrote an article entitled
'How to be an interesting person.' It expressed my interest at that
time in encouraging young people to express themselves and have
opinions rather than follow the 'schoolish' parrot-like repetition of
someone else's thoughts. The following are some of the ideas I
shared in that article:

> Sitting there reading this article, or half reading it, suppose
> somebody stopped you and said, 'Are you enjoying that?' It
> is not enough to say 'No' – or 'Yes' either! You must make
> yourself able to say why you do or do not like a thing. This
> is constructive criticism. A little child of two will admire a
> cheap, colourful, gaudy picture. He will simply say 'Oh!
> Nice!' Later, as a teenager, when shown the same picture,
> he will say 'Oh, it's awful.' When asked 'Why?' he answers,
> 'I dunno, it's just awful.' Is he an interesting person, do you
> think? No? Then you must make yourself put into words
> your opinions about things. If forced you could have said of
> that picture: 'It is too brightly coloured and the detail of the
> faces is very careless.' Such a comment not only sounds
> intelligent, but it pleases you and encourages you to think
> more. You are taking yourself in hand and beginning the
> task of making yourself an interesting person.
> At home at mealtime, when a film is being discussed or a
> TV programme is being 'cut to pieces', don't be afraid to
> say what you think about it. No need to be aggressive or
> insinuate that the rest of the family don't know what
> they're talking about. You will be much more effective if

you speak your views firmly but with good humour. Perhaps secretly, you enjoyed the film which your parents are saying was 'rot'. Well, up with you and say so, but not until you are able to say why you liked it. 'I thought the scenery was magnificent and that girl really can act; do you remember the part where she ...' Don't just sit there listening to the conversation, disagreeing, but afraid to speak up. You must push yourself to make that intelligent comment. If you give yourself a few such pushes the time will quickly come when you automatically have something to say which is worth listening to.

Instead of spending evenings pulling other people to pieces and listening vaguely to Radio Luxembourg pull yourself together for a change and listen critically to Radio Luxembourg. Think: 'Now what can I do from this minute on to make myself more interesting and attractive?' Then, 'What is it I like or dislike about this pop tune or that?' Driving through Killarney (or anywhere else), don't just look vaguely at the lakes, the trees and the mountains. Really see them. Thus can the prose of life become poetry. How could anyone describe Killarney with one word? Do you get the idea? You are making yourself an interesting person if you make yourself think critically and then put your thoughts into words ... It is a good thing to practise at home, on outings with the family, and among your friends. But don't go to the opposite extreme and forget to stop talking. Everyone must have his innings ... You will enjoy life much better if you look around, think and observe. You must also read. If you think your education ended or will end on leaving school, you are very much mistaken. School has only given you the beginning; now you must begin to apply what you have learnt and learn more as you go along. That doesn't mean that if you detested algebra you must still force yourself to study it or that you must sit up at night revising Latin verbs. No! But you must read the newspapers and be able to understand and discuss what is going on in the world. You read of a landslide or an earthquake in some distant part of Libya; be ready to get out the globe or atlas and find the spot. Such investigations whet your appetite for more. Read novels, digests, books relating to your favourite pastime or hobby. Go to plays, concerts and art exhibitions and test your ability to discuss intelligently what you have seen. If you, with your parents' help, are making a real effort to make yourself an interesting person, and develop your individuality; if you have trained yourself to think and form opinions, then you will not have the too-common complaint of teenagers about their dates: 'I didn't know what to talk about.'

Sunday Press, 14 April 1963

A question came in July 1979 from one young man which read:

Question: I am a young man of twenty-two. I have a good job and a good few friends. Life is not too bad except for one thing, when it comes to women I'm very shy. I could not ask a girl for a date because when we would be out I would start to shake and blush. Any time I went with a girl it was after I picked one up at a dance. I can't go to dances without a few drinks. This problem is really getting me down. If it keeps on I don't think I will ever be able to get married. Though it sounds like a stupid problem I feel it is ruining my life. Please give me some advice on what to do. I enclose £5 for the Conquer Cancer Campaign.

Signed: Depressed.

Answer: I am glad that you have friends and that there are experiences in life that you enjoy. This is a good start. Experiences in our lives with which we feel we are not coping can, at times, cast a gloom over the things that are working out satisfactorily ... I have been told many times that girls and boys get on much more easily together if they share a common interest. One lad, who wrote almost exactly as you have done, joined a group doing a summer project helping the elderly. The group of fellows and girls worked at renovating and decorating the homes of elderly people. Obviously their objective was not that of 'getting off' with one another. Rather were they sharing in creating something good outside themselves. So much so that they didn't even notice how well they were actually getting on with one another. You will need to be firm with yourself now. Seek out mixed activity in which you can become involved; things you would really like to do as well as things you feel human beings should do for one another. This may entail some research because if you live in a rural area you may have to be the one to start a club, project or sports or social group. Don't hang back from doing so. ... It can take courage and initiative to make the sort of changes that will get us out of a rut. So do start planning. I would be very glad if in a few months you would let me know how you got on. The courage with which you have tackled this difficulty in your life will be worth sharing with others to encourage them. If you opt out by using alcohol as a crutch you could be an alcoholic by then! The choice is yours – now. Thanks for the £5 received for the CCC (Receipt no. 5728)

On the ever recurring question of 'How far to go on a date?' I wrote in the following way in 1963:

Let's hope that understanding the nature of love a little better now, you will be slow to abuse it. It is useful to compare the appetite for sex with the appetite for food. Both are natural appetites. If you feel hungry you get food, you cook it and a climax of pleasure is reached when you eat it. Supposing you take the same example with a slightly different slant. You feel hungry so you buy a steak, cook it appetisingly and as you sit down to eat it your appetite has reached a climax. But this time you know that being on a serious diet, you are strictly forbidden meat! It was intensely stupid of you to have bought the steak to begin with. Now you must either be ill as result of breaking your diet or suffer the disappointment of a frustrated climax. Can you see the connection between this and the sexual appetite? The sexual appetite also has a natural climax which is followed by deep satisfaction. But the climax is morally forbidden outside marriage. Therefore it is intensely stupid for unmarried people to think that they can lovemake to a certain point and then find it easy to stop. No! Their natural appetite makes them desire the climax and the more intense their lovemaking the more difficult they will find it to resist. So do not do things or go to places which will tempt you to steal the pleasures intended only for married people. You can never steal the joy and satisfaction they have. You may have temporary natural excitement and pleasure but no lasting happiness and much remorse to follow ... Sexual control shows itself as 'the soul's mastery of the body' ... Love seeks to please and protect the loved one not to lead him or her to hell. It is not easy in the loveless world of today to stand up for your moral principles. But if you bravely accept the challenge you will certainly reap the reward.'

Sunday Press, 28 April 1963

By February 1979 the following type of letter was coming in to the Sunday Press column:

Question: We have been living together for some time. We couldn't afford to get married. Now my girlfriend is expecting and she has taken a dislike to me and wants to end our friendship. She wants to go ahead and have the baby. She says that she will have to continue working anyway and will have to find a way of having the baby looked after during the day. She says she's going to give the baby her name and just put a query rather than give my name as the father. Since I am the father and there is no doubt about that, I think I have a right to have the child named after me. Isn't it true that the father's name is automatically given to the child?

Answer: Since the girl is simply your common-law wife she can give the child her surname or yours, whichever she chooses. It is fairly obvious that since she doesn't now want to marry you, she would give the child her own surname. She does not have to register you as the father if she doesn't wish to. I feel from the details you've given me in your letter that her pregnancy came as a tremendous shock to both of you. It may well be better to make no definite decision regarding your relationship until the two of you have got used to this new situation. Your girlfriend may be reacting in shock. ... I have sent you details of counselling help available.

Questions about Confession quite often arrived in my mailbox. An example of one such from the seventies is as follows:

Question: It's over thirty years since I've been to Confession and I'm demented about this day and night. I've been praying for the courage to go and hundreds of times I've knelt outside the confessional and a terrible fear would come over me that I would not get absolution and so I would put it off again. I have prayed hard and have sent petitions and I go to Mass every Sunday, but I still can't get the courage. I'm one of a family who always lived up to their religion and I had a wonderful father and mother RIP. I just can't understand where I went wrong, but at one stage

in my life I went away to work and got in with people who
only thought of having a great time. I'm not trying to
blame them in any way. It was all my own fault. I just got
careless about my duties and soon was one of the crowd
just thinking about having a wonderful time. Then I got
fed-up of that way of life and after some time I came back.
… I felt so ashamed and disgusted with myself for all those
wasted years.

> Very Repentant Sinner, Belfast.

Answer: In all those years that you have wished to go to
Confession, your desire was to make things good with the
Lord and He loved that and has loved you all that time.
Those years have not been wasted. You have done many
things that were good and have really tried on occasions to
work up the courage to go to Confession. However you
developed a real anxiety over the matter and this led to fear
which increased your anxiety, and so on. This can happen
any of us in any aspect of our lives. The Lord understands
our very fragile human make-up, our responses to fear and
tension. It seems that your anxiety about Confession
became something of an obsession. There are a few things
you can do. Firstly, you could write to a priest confidentially,
explaining to him, much as you have explained yourself to
me, your difficulty about Confession and asking for an
appointment to see him. Alternatively, I could introduce
you to a priest and I could forward your full letter to him if
you gave me your permission to do that. If you would like
me to give you the name of a specific priest in Belfast
whom I feel would be most helpful to you, I shall be pleased
to do so if you send me a stamped-addressed envelope.

And a less tricky question (or is it more tricky?) which was asked
in a variety of ways as people got more weight conscious:

> **Question**: Angela, are you fat? If not you will probably not
> be able to answer my question, which is 'If you ever tried to
> lose weight, how did you do it?'
>   Middle-aged mother, Roscrea

> **Answer**: I'm about medium so I never did a serious weight-
> loss programme. But my advice is to eat less calorie-laden
> food, eat more sensible food, drink water, don't eat
> anything but fruit between meals and get as much exercise
> as you can. Don't aim for a huge change in weight
> immediately; be delighted at 1 lb a week. I must say that I
> wouldn't count the calories, I'd just eat less and walk more
> – if I could!

Sometimes in the *Sunday Press* column I gathered a few letters
together and made of them a composite article. It was a way of
dealing with more than the usual three questions in the space
allowed. The following is a part of the column of 20 November
1977, almost thirty years ago. It was a changing Ireland. A few
different headings separated the ideas which read as follows:

> **On Equal Choice Dances**: Anne points out that for too
> long girls had to sit around the disco or dancehall waiting to
> be asked up by a boy. She suggests that 'from the beginning
> to the end of the night, every person in the dancehall
> should have an equal right to select a partner for a dance.'
> How right! Why should we stick with the old social order
> which puts girls (who pay the same into the dance) into the
> position of having to wait to be chosen. Even then they may
> seldom be chosen by the men they would like to dance
> with. For everyone to be free to select a partner doesn't
> mean that everyone has to. Those who choose to sit and

wait may do so, but there would not then be the humiliation of sitting out because of no opportunity to dance. What we want now are DJs or dance organisers who'll make it known that their dances are 'Equal Choice' dances and then we need girls with the courage to make use of the opportunity offered them.

On Dating: Carol, in her comment, queries the right of the situation in which she (a Leaving Cert. student) has been dated a few times by Joe, whom she likes quite well. Now the group in the club have accepted that Joe and Carol are going together, so no other fellow will ask Carol out. All the time Carol prefers Mike, but what can she do? 'It's like being engaged' she says ruefully and asks 'Why can't a girl ask a fellow out, if she feels that they would get on well together?' Why not, indeed? We stick too rigidly and blindly to rules that have evolved that are not necessarily the best for people today. Groups of lads and girls should discuss this kind of situation and work out the truly fair and human approach. We are seeking not merely women's lib, but people's rights ... In a society where people clamour to be free we have an amazing set of dating rules which unnecessarily but effectively tie people down.

On fellows as friends: Which leads me on to the comments of Jane. Jane 'finds it impossible to meet fellows who are really interested in being friends with a girl.' She can't see a good marriage resulting from a friendship in which no more was shared than 'the disco, the pub, the match of the day and a bit of sex.' Behind the bravado, the big talk and the drink there are certainly men who want to be accepted understood and loved. So many boys are really shy and have less social education than girls. Some of them hide behind drink and loud talk and find sexual physical interaction easier than conversation. Girls can either go along with this, in which case real friendship may never develop even though these two may marry; or girls can follow their own promptings, tactfully taking control of the situation and encouraging the boyfriend to share more adventurous and interesting activities, more fun and more really human exchanges at the feeling and ideas level.

On marriage: Eithne takes up the point here when she says that 'Many girls nowadays have the good sense to decide that rather than marry any fellow who would turn up they would like to make an independent life for themselves… and remain single unless a really suitable partner turns up.' Nowadays girls can do just that, and if girls had an equal right to choose men friends then choosing to remain single would soon lose the old 'on the shelf' connotations.

On sex before marriage: Tess tells us that she went on the pill because her boyfriend wanted sex and she was 'afraid of losing him'. Margaret, too, asks about pre-marital sex. 'If they really loved each other would it be OK in that case?' Margaret adds that 'the girl might feel afraid of losing him.' Really Tess answers Margaret's question when she tells how, after she went on the pill, her boyfriend tired of the situation and now has other girlfriends. Broken-hearted she says 'How I wish I had listened to those people who said to keep sex for marriage.' The truth is that love is proved by sexual control until the commitment of marriage is made. The argument 'if we really love why not have pre-marital sex?' opens up the whole possibility of confusing love with infatuation and of exploitation in the name of love. It is amazing what can seem justifiable in the thrill of the moment. We need the clear unambiguous moral rule to save us from ourselves.

On rape in marriage: Kathy points out how far we are from real understanding of love when she asks 'Why, when rape is made such a serious thing before marriage, is it condoned within marriage?' The simple answer is that rape (forcing another person to have sexual intercourse) is an offence against the law of God. People will have to answer to God for such unloving.

On men's feelings: Right through these comments there was a note of longing for acceptance, understanding and affection. It is not only women who feel such longing. Perhaps men suffer more deeply since they go to greater lengths to disguise their loneliness. We have been conditioned to think that men shouldn't cry, but cry they do, deep inside themselves and their inner pain breaks out in behaviour such as drunkenness, wife-beating, aloofness from the family to whom they can't get close. Often a man's callous behaviour is the distortion of the crying that is going on inside him.

On friendship: Madge speaks of her terrible loneliness and depression. She feels that friends tire of you when you are not well. She needs even one friend who will stay with her during this difficult time. Each of us could stop here and ask ourselves if Madge is the prototype of someone whom we have neglected. Perhaps, Madge, you'll tell even one of your old friends how you are feeling and ask their help in getting your life going again. Most people are not basically cold and uncaring, but simply thoughtless and they can feel at a loss with a depressed friend ... At the same time keep the door of your own heart open. Let the love that certainly is there go out to other people through your cheery smile, your kind word, your listening ear.

On the Church: Finally, Nuala tells us that she thinks the Church seems to remain aloof from the day-to-day human pain, not teaching us to achieve that intimacy with Christ

that seems to bring serenity and hope. Nuala, I think each of
us needs to become more sensitive to the heart of the Gospel
message. Each of us who is Christian is personally
responsible for getting to know Christ better. If you were the
fan of a pop-star, you would try to get a full picture of the
kind of man he is. You would read avidly about him, what he
does, what he says, what has been said of him. You would
treasure some of the particularity endearing insights. If we
see Christ as the only leader challenging enough to follow
we will, likewise, seek to know him better and better. We
will learn to communicate with him in prayer and be with
him in silence. 'In the crook of his arm we will lie to rest.'
And when we are at our lowest we will hear him say again,
as he said to the little child who had died, 'Little girl, I say
to you, arise' and he took her by the hand and she got up.
Deeply sensitive to ordinary human needs, he said to the
family, 'Give her something to eat.'
Sunday Press 20 November 1977

Grey sky and fairy-lights, Christmas trees and cribs. That time
of year had come around again. Letters from the *Sunday Press*
dwindled as the Advent journey progressed. I was able to give time
to other things. I had, for years had the habit of doing much of my
Christmas shopping in the summer sales. Down from the attic
came purchases made six months previously. Friends were
horrified at the idea of thinking about Christmas in mid-summer,
but I thought happily about the enjoyment I had got from the
bargains I'd won when the shops were relatively quiet and
inexpensive, the weather frost free and, again, *Sunday Press* readers
distracted by their holidays.

One letter came in December 1973. It was a question that had
often come to my mind. It read 'Our eldest child is four this year
and we are wondering about whether or not to have Santa Claus.
If we start it now it may be very difficult to continue – things are
so expensive nowadays. Yet it would be a pity if the children had

to do without Santa Claus. He meant so much to us when we were kids. What should we tell her about him or should we leave the whole subject closed? If we don't have Santa Claus, she may feel that he doesn't come to our house but goes to every other house. So it's awkward.'

My answer then was as follows: Santa Claus is based on the story of St Nicholas and it is a story which you can tell very dramatically to even a small child of four: St Nicholas was a very good bishop. He is in heaven now and we call him Santa Claus (say 'St Nicholas' quickly and it turns into Santa Claus). When he was on earth he gave gifts to children who had nothing around Christmas time. Talk to the children imaginatively about this bishop setting out in the snow and leaving surprises in the various houses for the poor children.

We still remember St Nicholas and during the weeks of Advent the children can intercede with him in a simple prayer such as this, 'Please, St Nicholas, if I'm a very good child will you ask God to make Mammy and Daddy have enough money to put some little gifts in my stocking on Christmas night?'

Having them pray this way you make them aware that St Nicholas (Santa Claus) is now in heaven and very close to God and will speak to Him on their behalf. If they are very good and kind, God will make Mammy and Daddy able to put some little gifts in their stocking.

Yes, I do understand how much they love a stocking and I think their pleasure in it can be retained if we present Santa Claus in the way I have suggested. Some parents wonder how they can explain all the various 'Santas' that are found around town. I think the best thing here is to explain that these are good men who simply remind us of St Nicholas who is in heaven. Children enjoy the fact that people dress up and pretend to be other people, so you won't be taking the joy away by making this sort of explanation.

At another time I suggested keeping the 'stocking gifts' small so that if our financial situation was tight the stocking wouldn't be a huge worry.

At one stage when I was about six and was wondering about Santa, I lay keeping myself awake so that I would prove that it was Santa, not Daddy, who visited the nursery. A tingle of excitement filled the calm night. I heard the landing floor creak; the door opened gently throwing a light on the wall close by. To my amazement I saw the shadow of a hooded figure with a beard. I closed my eyes tightly, not wanting to be discovered to be awake. There was a glow in my heart as my secret doubts were dispelled. There was a rustle at the end of the bed and in a short time the door closed quietly. Now I knew so I could tell other children what I had seen … Daddy never did anything by halves! And, of course, Santa is as real as the tales we weave around a saint with a very unusual role. What a pity if we get him out of proportion in the Christmas story.

Back to the *Sunday Press*; I got greetings from clients who had been helped. In gratitude some sent money for charities. I usually wrote an article for the *Sunday Press* issue nearest Christmas to mark a very different Sunday. I illustrate the great goodwill of readers when, in answer to a little poem 'Christmas Pleading' which I wrote in Advent 1971, thousands of pounds were sent to my column responding to the need of the Pakistani people.

Christmas Pleading

On Christmas Day a knock at the door,
'It's Santa again' the children cried.
But it was a girl of twelve, not more,
A babe in arms and a brother of four,
Behind them men and women galore,
Children whimpering, cold and sore,
Hollow-eyed, hungry, silently pleading
'It's loving and warmth and food
They're needing',
Said the girl.

The people surged forward into the hall,
'They'll knock down our crib'
The children cried;
We heard them panic, we saw them fall
Crushing us and each other against the wall.
'For God's sake feed us'
Their voiceless call.
'How can we tell them it's Christmas for all?'
Hollow-eyed, hungry, silently pleading,
'It's loving and warmth and food they're needing,'
Said the girl.

Our cosiness, peace and comfort have died
'Please make them happy'
The children cried,
'Lord, I have opened the door too wide,
I want You to find me a place to hide
One family alone cannot stem this tide,
Our house is too small for them all inside, if
You'd sent but a few we'd have certainly tried
But it's no kind of life with these hundreds to guide.'
Hollow-eyed, hungry, silently pleading,
'It's loving and warmth and food they're needing',
Said the girl.

Turkey and pudding and hot mince pies,
'Give them our Christmas,'
The children cried.
Outstretched hands and beseeching eyes,
Have our claims that we love them largely been lies?
Have we closed our ears to their anguished cries?
'Remember I'm in them' the Lord replies
Hollow-eyed, hungry, silently pleading,
'It's loving and warmth and food they're needing',
Said the girl.

The family got together to help me in a massive drive to acknowledge and list the contributions. This was one of the times in which I felt a great sense of being backed up by so many *Sunday Press* readers.

15
Highs and Lows

As an asthmatic in the days before inhalers were perfected, I spent quite a few sessions in hospital. Things kept ticking over, but illness did interrupt the flow of home and work. Indeed, when my father had died in 1965 (he was sixty-six), I had a strange reaction: we were all in my home in Rathgar on the night of Dad's sudden death. Numbers of relatives and friends had arrived and we were busy serving tea and sandwiches when at about 10.30 p.m. Mary said to me 'You're looking a bit funny.' Funny? I looked in a mirror and saw that there was a rash on my face. I whispered to Peter that we'd better go home. So we drifted quietly off. Preparing for bed, I discovered that the rash covered my whole body like a map of the world. Next morning my eyes were too swollen to open properly and I had a massive attack of asthma. I was unable to go to my father's funeral and was brought into hospital where I had to stay for a couple of weeks. During the 1960s I had a few hospitalisations for the asthma until I finally got suitable cortisone medication. On the face of things, the *Sunday Press* column kept going with my photo showing a calm exterior, but I was paddling like mad beneath the surface. In 1970 I had another session in hospital to have my gall-bladder removed.

In 1973 I had a serious car accident resulting in two fractures of my jaw, flattened nose requiring rebuilding, a fractured foot, whiplash to my neck, spine pain, a torn eye-lid and multiple other abrasions and bruising. Here's how it happened: on a narrow, winding road in Co. Wicklow a car came in the opposite direction around a bend. I mounted the bank to avoid impact. The car went on, but my car bumped down off the bank. With no seat belts at that time, I hit my head off the metal surround of the sun-roof and knocked myself out. (That's a great ad for seat belts!) The car was stopped by impacting with a tree. My friend suffered a broken rib and severe bruising. A passing motorist brought us to a Wicklow doctor where I spoke to Peter on the phone. Thence to hospital in Dún Laoghaire. Don't forget, it was Peter's car that was now a write-off on that side road in Wicklow. He was so good about that. His brother brought him to meet me in the hospital. They didn't recognise me! The first time in hospital that I was able to look in a mirror I realised that I looked more like Queen Victoria in her later years than like myself. I was in hospital for some weeks. In a sense it was something of a rest. The *Sunday Press* had been very busy. I kept the column going from my hospital bed. Then, as result of the car accident, I began to have back problems which culminated in my having to wear a surgical collar. Eventually I had a back operation and a disc removed.

I was able to keep my newspaper column going, but I realised that help was needed over the whole scope of my work. So in the middle of it all, I made a significant decision: I decided to find people interested in the letter-counselling apostolate and train them with the help of some concerned and highly qualified experts in a few different fields. Thus would ease the log-jam of *Sunday Press* letters be dealt with. At least this was my optimistic plan. For this I needed an office, equipment, a regular secretary, money to pay her and the rent plus, if possible, a little car to get hither and thither from home. The whole project was daunting. But after praying and with some encouragement, I got going.

'If you want something done, ask a busy person.' With that phrase in mind I approached the late Fr Peter Lemass who together with Fr Joe Dunn had laboured with me on a TV documentary about my work to date, which was presented by

Radharc. (How old-fashioned that all looks now). Fr Peter was chaplain to the Brothers of Charity in Terenure. The brothers were debating the use of a house in Terenure which they had used for students. They agreed to rent it to me for a very generous and nominal rent pending any other decision about it. Delightedly, I accepted their very kind offer. My great social worker friend and I accessed about a dozen people who might be interested in training for the work of ghost writing for me and thus reducing the mountain of mail. Of course their work would be voluntary.

We gathered together a really fine group of people. The Jesuit Fathers in Rathfarnham had given us room in which to meet. I talked with these people about the proposed work. We held a simple selection conference for the participating people. Some felt that the work was not for them. Others agreed on a period of training. I had written rules for counselling by letter.

These guidelines were taken one by one at the meetings of Christian Counsel, they were discussed and examples of their application were made in carefully reading letters together. Individuals in the group made suggested responses. Letters for homework were distributed. Our guidelines were as follows:

GUIDELINES FOR COUNSELLING BY LETTER

1. Read the letter very carefully; however brief it is, there is a thinking, feeling person behind it.

2. Note inconsistencies. Jot down your own reactions.

3. Pick up the emotional as well as the intellectual content of the letter.

4. Accept client as he/she was at the moment that person wrote.

5. Do not exhibit confusion, e.g. 'It's terribly difficult for me to know what to say'. What the client needs is clarification.

6. Be non-judgemental. We have no right to judge the client or anyone he or she writes about.

7. Limit advice-giving to facts, e.g. acquainting the client with services. Never say 'If I were you I wouldn't…'

8. The client must feel your genuine interest in him/her as a loveable person.

9. Avoid the use of language/jargon that might not be understandable to the client.

10. Respect the client's right to make his/her own choices and decisions. Endeavour to activate the client's potential for self-direction.

11. Reassure the client about your commitment to confidentiality.

12. Avoid excessive emotional involvement. Aim to help client become self sufficient.

13. Don't offer undue or premature reassurance, such as 'Everything will be fine.' It may not.

14. Don't be afraid to convey the 'ordinariness' of yourself, e.g. 'I know what you meant when you said how tired and impatient you were with the children; I get like that too. Perhaps we should...'

15. A high level of accurate empathy gets the message across to the client that 'S/he really knows what I'm talking about.'

We met there and in my home. I should, I suppose, have seen a red light early on. Now I had the job of training people to do this work as well as continuing to actually keep on doing it myself.

When the Terenure house was at last ready for use by us, we arranged to meet one evening per week for training and discussion. I advertised for a secretary for what was now a registered charity called 'Christian Counsel'. I wanted people to know that the counselling offered would be from a Christian perspective. We were blessed to get a young woman, Mary, who was eminently suited – if not over-qualified – for the job. She took over the setting up of a well-run office. When I think of it now, she had great courage and selflessness in taking on what was an unpredictable future where, to begin with, we had no money. Mary initiated fund-raising. We invited people to be patrons, among whom were the Archbishop of Dublin, Most Rev. Dr Dermot Ryan; Sr M. Jude Walsh, Mother General, Medical Missionaries of Mary; Mrs Mercy F. Simms; Lady Wicklow; Dr Charles Smith, MRCPL, MRC Psych, DPM; Mr Sean Bedford. I wrote to the Vatican for a blessing on our endeavour, which I received. I had high ideals, hadn't I? Can ideals be too high?

With the help of Redemptorist students a leaflet was produced introducing us and describing our plans. I would have been quite well known at that time having run the column plus having been on a few TV and radio programmes. Christian Counsel was launched with a Mass in our office and a little party to follow. A good response resulted from our fund-raising, including donations from bishops, parish clergy, some religious orders and a fine mix of lay people. It was an encouraging start and enabled me to pay the main expenses. At just about that time a little miracle occurred which further encouraged me to feel that Christian Counsel was the will of God: I had for years a prize bond about which I had almost forgotten. One morning I received an uninteresting looking formal letter. Well? Imagine my surprise when I found that it was telling me that my only prize bond had won a prize of a few thousand pounds. At last I would be able to have a little car. So I bought my first car – a little blue Fiat Bambino. I was thrilled with it. I was able to go back and forth to the office and to work appointments without depending on the buses.

As the training of the group progressed, the work load seemed to increase. I decided that I had to vet letters written by the trainees. I couldn't, I thought, let them sign the letters as recipients might feel let down and even that there was a breach in confidentiality in my giving their letter to another person. So as they took one or two letters a week to work on, I had to continue at my usual pace as well as correcting the letters of the trainees and explaining and discussing the corrections as part of the training. So, at this point, I actually had increased my work-load – temporarily, I hoped. I began to wish that we could encourage people to write 'Dear Christian Counsel' so that at the conclusion of our training course, each new letter-writer could be responsible for his/her replies. I should have followed through this thought for the privately answered letters. But someone pointed out that all the correspondents might then write specifying that they wanted me to reply because they felt they knew me.

My health difficulties were beginning to cause me to feel exhausted and depressed. At first a restful weekend restored me and I continued with the talks in schools, the *Sunday Press* and the training. But when I met the group on Tuesdays, the meetings tended to start with chat and laughter whilst I was impatient to get along with business.

On the home front, two of our daughters were married in 1977 and '79 with all the joy and planning these entailed. Each of our four daughters decided on the type of wedding she and her boyfriend liked best. We decided to give each of them the same amount of money as was then required for a normal white wedding. Then they could do as they wished with the money. Some settled for a small wedding and the rest of the cash in hand, others differently. That worked very well. My own parents had arranged a big formal wedding and reception for me and I would have preferred a different type of event. I was determined to give our daughters 'carte blanche' in their arrangements. Incidentally, it made it all easier for ourselves. So, there was a lot going on in our home as well as some school days, while Christian Counsel (CC) was finding its feet. We set up a booklet of 'Sample Letters' for the trainees (most of those used were anonymous). We used these for discussion on the Tuesday nights and applied our counselling rules to them. Television, and the more secular and materialistic magazines and papers, had become an enormous influence in our country and on our children. New-style problems connected with different approaches to life, were turning up all the time.

The members of Christian Counsel were probably finding my perfectionist scrutiny of their efforts trying and somewhat discouraging. With hindsight, I can see that. I never liked the perfectionist streak in myself and it always got worse when I was busy. My horizons were too wide. With Mary at the helm the office organisation was taking on a clear outline. Her organising abilities were far greater than mine. We built up a small library of relevant books for our own use and made a booklist to send to correspondents underlining the books that might be of particular help in each one's situation. We also formalised our 'Helpers' List' with the names of people from all over Ireland who had so kindly offered to help any client in their area whom we might refer to them. Then we familiarised ourselves with clubs and classes in Dublin which we listed also with a view to clients who were lonely and felt that they had no social life; we explored the Social Services available. So we learned a great deal as Christian Counsel mushroomed. Each year we prepared an Annual Report to send to benefactors. I had the help of an experienced and brilliant priest in doing this. We also received occasional cheques from members of the public. So we kept within our financial parameters. My helpers were, bless them, voluntary.

But in the second half of the 1970s I felt myself less and less able for the expansion that was taking place. I had had a hysterectomy. Menopausal women can feel exhausted, depressed and cranky at times. Sometimes when I was in bad mood at home one or other of my daughters would sing or hum, 'Must be meno, must be meno, must be meno, men-o-pause!' (to the tune of the Santa Claus song). That used to make us laugh. At times I was laid-up and Mary and the group continued to hold the fort.

After a continued period of training I read a ghost-letter written by one of the group. I felt that she was not reflecting the way of responding that I thought to be necessary and according to the rules. I had been thinking that she was not gifted in the letter-writing aspect of counselling. So I wrote to her and told her that I didn't think that she was suited to this particular work. I should have met her, but I felt neither the emotional energy nor the courage to do that. Well! She was very angry, as was a friend of hers in the group. They both resigned. The cracks were beginning to become apparent and I felt unable, physically and emotionally, to shore up the weakening edifice. The dream was slipping into a nightmare for me. I should have said quite openly to the group that I felt myself becoming burned-out. Then we could have discussed the best way to cope with that. But I didn't do so. We struggled on. The remaining members did Trojan work. Each was beginning to identify the kinds of letters they felt best able to cope with using their particular expertise. For example, Michael did the business-type letters, Gay, the marriage problems, Lilian the young people's questions, Séan the theological letters, Aideen the more general letters, Gill the letters where psychiatric referral seemed needed and so on. But I was still in the position of leadership and badly needed to hand over. Yet I was the one who was heading the column and doing the schools' work and at that time there was no-one feeling ready to follow 'my act'. I had so much experience by then. I had tried delegating, but not considered how we would organise the next leader of Christian Counsel. Strangely, Christian Counsel, in spite of our hard work, had produced more headaches than help for me. I simply did not have any experience in setting up a group and I was no longer able to keep it all up. I was confronted with as many problems as were my clients.

The group tailed off gradually at the end of the 1970s. Likewise, by 1980 the Sunday Press column fizzled to a close. The media in Ireland were becoming secularised. My sort of spiritually-based response to problems began to lose popular ground, which was understandable. I had a good innings, now I was feeling too exhausted and low to continue the full role.

That's how that initiative folded up. I had a deep sense of failure, feeling that I had let people down. Summer 1980 was coming and I anticipated with a mixture of pleasure and sadness the holiday and the decision time that lay ahead. What next? was the key question. For the first time I considered full retirement. But I was to talk regularly of retirement and then revive myself for still a few years. When the autumn came I waited to see what might happen in the schools. I was advised 'When the river dries up, then is the time to stop.' But invitations continued to flow in and I decided to continue with those situated relatively close at hand. This I did. I also wrote occasional articles for journals, papers and magazines. I have always loved writing and it comes quite easily to me – even still. Having kept a personal journal, I have continued to do so. I find it to be a way of looking at what is going on inside oneself. When we moved house in the eighties I destroyed most of my back journals. There was no room in the smaller house for old memories. But I continue to write each day. I began to do a little art work; just making little greeting cards for my own use. I love this hobby. I redesigned my sessions with parents and made new transparencies for overhead projectors for both parents and children. So, in the 1980s and into the 1990s I continued, in spite of three further house moves, to go to the parents' and children's sessions in schools. I counselled privately any parents from 'my' schools who came to me for help. I discovered that failure can be humanising and that, as Henri Nouwen put it, 'It often happens that the patient is exactly the right plaster for the doctor's sore spot.' The schoolchildren were therapy for me.

Some lay teachers were interested in having meetings with me regarding the idea of their giving sex and relationships education themselves in their schools. Some were inclined to say of me, 'You're a once off, a difficult act to follow.' I'd had a good headstart. Others who were of the next generation in their way of life, believed in talking of 'sin' as 'inappropriate behaviour' and considered that children should always feel 'comfortable' and be given choices. I still feel that 'right' and 'wrong' need to be spelled out rather than watered down to a sort of comfortable, unchallenging mediocrity. Choices, yes, but responsible choices can only be made when the moral dictates are understood. But everyone picks up ideas from reading, listening to others, reflecting and creating the approach that best suits their convictions. I thought the idea of teachers starting off Relationships and Sexuality Education for their own school could be very useful as, indeed, it proved to be in some cases. RSE is needed, but only if it is interwoven with the basic moral messages and parents are invited to share.

I continued writing letters to people who had met me through the *Sunday Press* and continue, even still, to write to me. I enjoyed the creative aspect of house moves and it was useful to let go of much of our collective rubbish as well as some of our well-loved furnishings. But it is an exhausting activity, isn't it? Over the years for what seemed to be very good reasons, we changed house seven times!

This phase of life they call 'the menopause' is also termed 'the change of life'. It was certainly that for me. I was saddened by the closure of Christian Counsel – my five-year old dream. I had thought it would be a letter-counselling initiative that would take off in centres throughout the country! That wasn't to be. True, Ireland had changed beyond recognition during the sixties and seventies, yet there are many problems that will always be with us and for which we need the comfort of a helping person. Some people in the past found that writing them down was the easiest method of sharing their problems. By the 1980s and '90s people had less time and, perhaps a diminishing sense of generosity about doing voluntary work. Letter-writing was becoming a lost art because of all the new communications technology. I think that is a great loss; no e-mail, text message or even phone call can replace the intimacy of a letter from a friend. But people have so little time nowadays. In the 1960s we thought that with all the modern technologies and 'mod cons', people would have, perhaps, too much spare time in the future. We imagined that a modern problem might be learning how to make the best use of spare time. That was a problem that disappeared and, instead, we now have the most stressed generation ever. Along with the stress came a loss of familiar spiritual and moral values. There is a big push in medical and scientific circles to artificially prolong life as its natural end draws near and to get rid of life at its dawning. Fewer people have worked out any ultimate purpose for living. We note with deep sadness the increase in suicides. A clarion call rings in my ears once again. We must respond to the challenge 'in season and out of season' right to the end. But how?

16
A Day of Reflection

After some time, alongside the RSE, I sought to develop the 'Relationship-with-Christ' aspect of Education in Relationships by having a special 'Day of Reflection' (a mini-Retreat, really) with the children. During these days we 'walked beside Christ'. We were the Emmaus disciples. We considered parables, role-played some of these, tried to capture the feeling and meaning of these situations and to identify with Him and His companions. I remember talking about the visit Jesus paid to Martha and Mary. The girls role-played the scene. Mary sat at His feet and listened to Him while Martha was busy in the background. The children felt sorry for Martha, but one girl commented 'Why didn't she get them something like an old-fashioned pizza and she wouldn't have had to be away from Him so long?' After our chats on events in Christ's life, we gave time to sitting quietly with Him eyes closed, looking at him, 'seeing' what He looked like. His brown skin and dark hair. His garment, his sandals, the warmth of His expression, hearing what His voice was like. The children were wonderfully relaxed for these sessions and most found them refreshing – even exciting. In conclusion each of us wrote to Christ, expressing anything we wished to share with Him. These letters were burned at the Offertory of the Mass, the smoke signifying the content of each letter rising to God. (If we could not do that, the children trusted me to burn their letters at home without looking at them.

This I did.) How I loved these sessions. There was a very special feeling as we shared them. I recall a girl, all aglow, saying to me that she felt she had 'Never met Christ before'.

Such basic questions arose as 'Why did God send Christ anyway?' I often told them a little story that illustrates God's purpose in translating God's self into human terms:

> A farmer looked out of his window on a snowy winter day. It was bitterly cold outside. There in his yard were three little birds. One was obviously injured. The other two fluttered around their hurt little companion. The farmer said to his wife 'Those birds will die in that cold.' He decided to open the big door of his barn where the birds could go into the hay and be protected from the icy wind. So out went the farmer and opened the barn door. He tried to usher the little birds in. But they were frightened of him and fluttered around even more anxiously. So the farmer left them and went back sadly to the kitchen where he shrugged and said to his wife 'No good, they don't understand what I want. If I could be one of them I could explain in the way they would understand. Then they would follow me into the warmth.'

The birds didn't know that the farmer cared for them. Likewise, many people feared and misunderstood God until Christ came. God became a person in Jesus Christ so that we would understand His message, follow Him and be saved ultimately from the cold and ills of the world.

Just as the people of Christ's time enjoyed stories, so, I've discovered, do the children today. We discussed the deep significance of each little tale. Often they role-played an episode from daily life which helped in the live application of the Christian message. Questions followed: Is Christ's way easy? Is it the way I want to live? Will it give meaning to life? Sometimes I asked the children to pretend for a minute that each of them is the Great

Creator; what would be their ten basic requirements of the people they created if there was to be happiness? ('Be honest!') The children were always quick to list justice, love, honesty, generosity and so on. We then looked at God's ten commandments to see if they fitted in to our ideas of the basic needs of people who were to be happy and at peace. Were God's requirements easy?

'How could Our Lady have got pregnant without sex?' one boy of twelve enquired. A hand shot up. 'Yes Conor?' I prompted. 'The Holy Spirit zapped her,' explained Conor. That's how they talk!

Sixth-class children are about to be confirmed. Confirmation should mean making a personal decision at a significant stage in life, to opt for the Christian life. God has left us free to choose and right through life we find ourselves making what can be the very hard choice of opting courageously for Love (against greed, power, excessive possessions, bullying, gossip, side-lining people). Sadly, many children are confirmed without awareness that this decision is one of the greatest life decisions they will ever make. Parents have a big role to play in encouraging and living-out at home this life-long decision for Christ. Sometimes I passed around little cards on which were pictures of some good act someone was doing. When the music stopped, the card you held showed a kind, brave or honest act that each particular child had to try to accomplish in the next few days, for example, 'If you think someone looks nice, tell them; if they look sad, cheer them.' Some of the exercises were left out if the discussion flowed in a fruitful way. The Spirit guided us, I'm sure.

One exercise they did with me, when a garden was available, was to go out at the break and each bring back some natural, ordinary, beautiful or interesting thing they found underfoot in the garden. They brought back those lovely skeleton leaves of winter, a coloured stone, a daisy, a piece of soft moss, a leaf of unusual shade or shape. I had an empty tray on which these finds were arranged making a delightful collage. The message was: 'We might never have seen or been touched by these things had we not looked carefully. So this trayfull of the simple and lovely things

that are so often trodden on the ground will represent the down-
trodden people of the earth the beauty of whom so few people
see.' The richest use of imagination is to give insight into the
beauty of the world. We then planned to offer our tray-full to
God, either at the Offertory of the class Mass or in a little private
ceremony. Thus are our blessings blessed. If we were to have a
Mass, we got together and planned the music, the symbols, the
offerings and readings. The girls really enjoyed their participation.
This seems to tell me something important about involvement,
flexibility and listening courteously to the ideas of the young.

Before the Mass I explained the Eucharist-nourishment for the
soul. They have forgotten so much since First Holy Communion.
Then there was a period of quiet. The children thought privately
of any worry they had been having – a cloud in their lives. We
imagined that, attached to each of our clouds was a string. We
clenched between thumb and finger the imaginary string so that
each cloud hovered above its owner's head. Then, in our hearts we
offered our needs to the Father knowing that He would do what is
truly best for each of us. At the tinkle of my little bell each let go
of her 'string' and we pictured letting go our worries to God. The
clouds soared up to heaven. Then we thanked Him. We are always
heard. I pointed out to them that we can do such a little exercise
at any time. In God's good time the answers to our worries will be
made clear. I told the children:

> A little boy prayed to be able to take his teeth in and out the
> way his Grandad did. Next morning he tried his teeth, but
> they were firmly stuck. 'God doesn't answer,' he
> complained. Later in life he was very glad that his teeth had
> remained in place. God had done what was best for him.

Gradually, over the decade of the nineties, schools had less time to
give. Our 'Days of Reflection' were shortened to an hour or not at
all. School timetables were overloaded. Parents seemed to want
the children to have more of the nuts and bolts of sex education.

Could it be that in our pragmatic world we are losing the magic of
creativity in everyday education?

'Why do you bring God or prayer into it so often?' I've been
asked that question about my response to the letters or the basic
orientation of my talks. Prayer has become something of an
unmentionable embarrassment for some people over the years
since I was young. Others consider that prayer is for simple folk
not for the sophisticated, the 'cool' or, of course, the secularist.

Long ago people in Ireland quite readily said 'Thank God',
'Please God', 'God bless him', 'God willing'. It may have been a
habit, a turn of phrase used by many people or a genuine prayer.
But it was not sneered at nor carefully avoided as it can be today.
People who made the Sign of the Cross outside a church were
saluting the Person of Christ within. The majority of Catholics did
so in my childhood. Religious pictures and statues were honoured
in the home. Nowadays, you will have noted, if people being
interviewed on radio or television are asked 'Are you religious?'
they almost always begin their reply by saying, 'Not really, but ...'.
Has it become shameful to say a simple 'Yes' to that question?
Clearly, the first commandment of God puts honouring God in
primary place. What are the 'strange gods' honoured today?
Money, power, possessions, status, these are the most important
things bowed to today in western society. The philosophy of
individualism (or 'me'-ism) has made us greedy. Many people are
afraid of looking too closely at the idea of putting God first. It
could cause us to have to change our lives too much people fear.
'Don't be seen to be Catholic' is a new interpretation of the Equal
Status Act, which bans discrimination. In that case even the
recognisable pastor, nun, priest or rabbi on the street could be said
to be a source of division. 'Better,' some say, 'to hide your light
under a bushel.' But that is not what Jesus said.

There is a deep yearning for God and for the spiritual planted
in the heart of every person. People have often expressed to me
their longing to share, however incoherently, that yearning. It
often seems that there is no-one with whom to have such a

sharing. The loud and active presence of a secular media can drown out the call of Christ unless we speak or write to one another of Him. Karl Rahner wrote the following significant words:

> When things are going well we manage fine without Him. But when the nest of our content is shaken by the rough winds, then we expect the Kingdom of Heaven, so blissfully ignored up to now, to come immediately to our aid so that we can, once more, be in the happy position of having no need of Him.

17

The Queen Bee

1999

There were children milling around the school yard, hopping and screaming like magpies. I was looking for the main door. Two anxious little girls, one ponytailed the other afro-styled, hovered around, nudging each other and looking at me. I smiled at them. 'Are you looking for someone?' I asked. 'Are you the sex lady?', 'Yes, I suppose I am,' I replied. They were relieved. They had been sent to pick me up 'at the door' but I was at the wrong side of the yard. They were delighted that the mistake was mine. Little Miss Afro asked 'Do you do "the birds and the bees?"' Miss Ponytail interjected 'Mammy said you're the Queen Bee.' The three of us laughed. Clearly another day with sixth class primary schoolgirls had already begun.

On reaching the classroom a cheerful young teacher greeted me and spoke a bit about the day while simultaneously letting out bellows at the children to get them into some kind of order. Having glanced around I asked if the overhead projector was easily got at. I had asked the Principal to have it available as I had some illustrations to share with the children. 'Miss O'Grady has it in her room,' responded Miss Cheery. I asked if someone could bring it down for me. Miss Cheery doubted if Miss O'Grady would part with it 'this being Tuesday'. 'She's big into it, uses it every Tuesday,' she offered by way of explanation. I asked if there was another projector and was told 'Well, there's the old one.' Eventually 'the old one' was trundled in by a gaggle of girls all of whom wanted to show me how well it worked if you put a 'phone book under the left side. The screen was the stained classroom wall. 'Are you all right now?' beamed Miss Cheery assuring me that she would be in the staff room if anything went wrong. She gave a final shout at the children, 'Remember what I said' she told them ominously. 'Yes Miss' they chorused. Off she went, and it was over to me. I just stood quietly and looked at the scene with what I hoped was a friendly gaze. Curious about my stillness the children shushed one another. Silence came and I began what promised to be another energetic day. Echoing the words of an ancient children's radio programme I asked, 'Are you all sitting comfortably? Then we'll begin.'

'Guess what!' I said. 'We're going to begin with a prayer.' I knew that they wouldn't expect that. I asked them if they understood my reason for that. They were a bit uncomfortable and looked around at one another. I waited until one girl spoke, 'Is it because we're in Confirmation class?' she suggested haltingly. 'Well done, that's certainly a very good reason.' I told them that I was confirmed and that I well understood our need for the wisdom and understanding, gifts of the Holy Spirit, when we are starting on an important venture. For that was what we were about to do. Some of them nudged and looked heavenwards. 'Love and sex are an adventure into life,' I continued. There was a concealed giggle at those significant words. Interest began to take over. I prayed spontaneously about all of us there and our need to invite God to be present with us for our day. 'Love and sex were designed by You, God, so You are the best one to help us to understand.' We launched into the day.

In this era questions are readily asked from the floor, but there is a question box for anyone who prefers to write her question. Time was also put aside for private chats with me where an individual girl or a couple of friends might want to discuss something confidential. All of these opportunities for questioning were taken up right from the start. I made sure that any mobile phones were turned off. Not all schools have strict rules about mobiles. Texting can take place under the table and bullying by text messages is a new aspect of that problem.

The questions for the question box were written any old way on scraps of paper torn from exercise books or jotters. Typical of these questions from the twelve-year-olds were the following: (I exclude the spelling mistakes here!)

What exactly is a homo? And a bisexual?

Is it OK to kiss a fella at our age?

Boys do things to us in the park, but I'm afraid to tell at home. What can I do?

What age can you start using condoms?

My mum never talks to me about growing up and things. What can I say to her?

I have no friends. People laugh at me in class. I feel stupid.

I go to discos and we 'meet' guys. I like that, but no fella asks me to go with him.

Will you talk more about what boys have when we have periods?

My dad drinks. I'm afraid of him when he's drunk. Can I talk to you?

How can a woman lose a baby? A baby is big.

What do lessies do? How do they get a baby?

What's a test tube baby?

In soaps they always have sex and they're not married. Nowadays everyone does.

I've never gone with a boy. I'd be afraid. Other people laugh at me so I pretend.

I don't really understand periods and the things people wear. Will you tell us more?

I wish I was allowed do the same as other people. My dad is old-fashioned.

I am always struck by the enormous influence of peer pressure, even worse for boys. At the break I might have had a mug of tea or coffee brought to me in the classroom when there is no other space to spare. All the girls left the room with the teacher and those who wanted to talk to me privately came back individually while I took my coffee. In a way, my having my 'cuppa' lent a homely air to the sharing. Outside the door there was often a group waiting to come in and arguing loudly about their place in the queue. Some teachers arranged it all better than others.

Catherine slipped tentatively into my room one morning. She was small and thin for her age with wispy fair hair. I often start by asking the child how she is finding the group sessions. That may be followed by my question 'Is there any bit that you find difficult because sometimes I think I may go too quickly?' Catherine replied 'The bit about condoms'. I waited for her to tell me what aspect troubled her. 'Well,' she said 'I found a packet of condoms beside Mum and Dad's bed.' 'And what were you thinking?' I asked her. 'I thought they shouldn't have them.' 'So?' I looked enquiringly at her, 'I took them and burned them.' said Catherine. I asked her why she felt that to be necessary and she replied that she thought people shouldn't use them. I explained that in the class group I had said that sex before marriage was not *the ideal* according to the teaching of the Catholic Church so, therefore, before marriage there should be no need for condoms. 'But, Catherine, you have no need to worry about your parents. As married people they will have thought out the best thing for them and will have come to the decision that seems wisest in their situation. It is a very private decision for married people and they will often talk with a doctor or counsellor about it. But no one interferes with that decision. So you have no need to worry about your parents.' She was so relieved. I found myself thinking how different was twelve-year-old Catherine's problem compared to the problems of even seventeen-year-olds thirty years previously.

Parents' marital status is often a cause for concern for youngsters today. In the middle of one class, extrovert Noelle put up her hand to ask a question: 'Angela,' she said, 'My Mam and Dad were married last Christmas holidays and I was a bridesmaid.' Then she added with hesitation 'Was that OK?' All the children were listening with interest. Certainly the teacher's job can be difficult. 'Was it a very exciting day?' I asked Noelle smilingly. She told us that it was lovely and mentioned the hotel in which the reception took place. 'And the family is very happy now?' 'Oh yes,' she said. 'Well, God is delighted when people marry and He wants families to be close to each other. Marriage, which God blesses, makes the bond really close so He must have been thrilled to share with you all on that day.' Noelle went on to say that she had brought photos to show me and everyone wanted 'a look'. I suggested that the photos should be left until our break time. I was thrilled for Noelle that they were such happy photos. Here again, we have the sort of situation that must be faced in the modern classroom.

Children worry much more about the possible divorce or separation of their parents than many people recognise. Even an unhappy relationship between the parents at home seems to be better in the eyes of many children than to have to face divorce or separation.

Such would be the progress of a school day from the late eighties to 2000. It is interesting to note the mixture of innocence, ignorance and lack of self-confidence that existed with senior students twenty years earlier compared to the often brash, information-saturated girls and boys of today. Children had time to be children in those days. Nowadays they are pressured into growing up and becoming sexualised before they have even reached the double figures in age. Yet there is also a healthy sense today that 'only in freedom can people direct themselves towards goodness.' If one is not free to be wrong then neither is one free to be right. But teaching the rules comes before driving the car.

Interestingly, the children responded well to spiritual values creatively presented and to the idea of relationship with Christ 'the invisible companion who is there for you throughout life.' When we grow to love Christ we become like the lover with the beloved, wanting to do what pleases Him. I find that simple human stories help children to work out the underlying message. I might begin a session with a stark statement, for example, 'This week I was at the funeral of a boy of twelve. (Silence). A guard of honour of his classmates lined the aisle in the church. They looked serious and were quiet. Some brushed tears aside. Yet many of them had bullied Tony mercilessly every day of his school life. Why? Because Tony was small and quiet, not good at sports and got headaches very often. God, who created Tony respected and loved him, but some of the lads judged and mocked him and called him cruel names. Now they looked silently at his weeping family. How do you think the boys felt inside themselves? (Wait for responses). How had Tony felt each day? His brain haemorrhage took him swiftly – what can those who bullied him do now? (Wait) You know, bullying is a sin. It is against God's law of love. All our lives we choose to be with God or against Him. It is a personal decision: You, Siobhán, you, Emma, You, Laura and I make that decision every day. Why do you think people bully? (Wait for response, listen, discuss and encourage.)'

Other times, perhaps when we are talking about physical development, a funny story fits in: a fellow went into a shop to buy his girl-friend a bra. Brave, wasn't he? Anyway he didn't know the size so the assistant tried to help him 'Would it be like two grapefruit?' she asked. 'Oh no, much smaller', said the fellow. 'Well, two pears?' the girl suggested. 'No, smaller still,' said the guy. The assistant tried again, 'Two eggs?' 'Yes,' said the relieved boy, adding 'fried eggs.' Stories produce all sorts of emotions, laughter, sympathy, fellow-feeling, seriousness – and that lovely feeling of relief at not being the only one who has worries or makes such mistakes. The girls always enjoyed when I shared with them some experience I had in my own life: 'Wait 'til I tell you a really cringe-making thing that happened to me...' brought 100 per cent attention.

From the eighties on most of my invitations were to spend days with sixth-class primary school children (eleven to thirteen-year-olds). Being subjected to TV, videos, internet, teen magazines necessitated their being well and sensibly grounded in facts and moral principles. In earlier decades there had been undue emphasis on sin, guilt and an angry punishing God. Now we have to find new ways to speak about God introducing them to a God of love, justice and forgiveness. Yet we have to avoid bringing them to the point where it doesn't really matter what one does because this 'soft' God will forgive anything – and no strings attached. I discussed such attitudes with the parents. The establishing of standards and values required a whole mix of approaches. During the eighties the parents were interested in such ideas. 'Without moral standards we would have chaos in society', most of us would have agreed. The secular society had not yet got a hold. We had to find the warm and acceptable way of giving the clear and unambiguous message to the children.

In the nineties, along with teacher, author and educator Francis McCrickard, I made two sex education videos, one for girls and one for boys. Facing a live class of girls, or even boys, was a much easier task. In the video-making there was a script, autocues and the director, producer and camera-men. Francis was a great asset, he was so at ease. I felt out of my element and quite nervous. These videos were to help parents at home and teachers in the classroom. It seems that they are still going strong. Strangely, the shyness that has always afflicted me in ordinary social groups was never there when I spoke to class groups and their parents. I felt secure and confident enough around my own subject, I suppose. I had got very used to it.

Thirty years ago it was usual for one girl from the class to give a vote of thanks to me as a visiting speaker. She might begin: Mrs Macnamara, on behalf of the class I would like to thank you …'. Nowadays, when the final bell rings there is often a mad rush for the door to catch the bus or a lift home. A few girls hang around chatting to me as I pack up my things. I remember Rebecca with the single dangling ear-ring, giving her personal vote of thanks: 'That was cool, Angela, You have to be pretty good to keep bums on seats around here.' We all laughed. Times have changed.

18

A Curtain is Drawn

We were told about Peter's incurable cancer some months before he died. In some ways I entered into his struggle against the death sentence. Possibly something could reverse the situation? Maybe even a miracle? But one day, while driving to the hospital, I was playing a cassette of psalms. They always have such a healing message. Loud and clear, one verse sprang out to me. I stopped the car and listened to it again:

> *Take, Lord, receive*
> *All is Yours now,*
> *Dispose of it wholly according to Your will.*
> *Give me only Your love and Your grace,*
> *That's enough for me,*
> *Your love and Your grace are enough for me.*

At that moment I knew that I must let go. There, on a lay-by on the N11, I opened my hands in a symbolic gesture. I shall always remember that spot on the road. While I prayed for strength, there was a sense of relief mixed with sadness. I played the psalm again as I was to do many times in the coming weeks. I recognised the moment of grace I had been given. That day, when I arrived at the hospital, I met the oncologist. He told me they had decided not to give Peter chemotherapy. It was too late to do anything for him.

Somehow that information fitted in with my earlier gesture of releasing my beloved husband to God. I had a strange sense of moving around in a dream. It was the beginning of the end. Now my unspoken response to Peter's every move was 'Farewell, my love, farewell.'

Christmas came and went. Candle-light whispered of endings, and gift-givings had a finality about them. Peter insisted on coming home for Christmas Day. I decorated and prepared more or less as we had always done together. He made such a brave effort to make it as normal as he could. But each of us was so aware of his condition as we tried to enjoy the gifts, eat the turkey and pull crackers.

I wasn't good at pretence. A couple of times I slipped out of the room to try to pull myself from the brink of tears. At one stage I saw Peter standing at the window looking out at his much-loved garden. I wondered what he was thinking. But he wasn't a man who would have wanted to be asked that question. We played some music that he and the girls had always enjoyed, and the tears came. The younger grandchildren, unsure of what was going on, played in a reserved way with new toys, their natural exuberance deflated. I can still feel my own mixed emotions and the sense of being unable to find the best way to be. So strange after forty-five years of spontaneous sharing.

January 9th, 1998. 'My husband is dead.' I had to write these words as though to convince of the message they contained. He was gone, my husband, friend, lover, companion and confidant. Peter, my rock, was no longer there. However strongly I believe in life eternal, I long for a husband whom I can touch and hold. Yet, I reflect, I have learned to have an intimate relationship with Christ whom I have never met. So now Peter is united with God, so can I learn to have a new relationship with him in that context? I have to wait and learn about that. Meanwhile, in faith, we must settle for the mystery.

My journal entry for 9 January 1998 reads:

My darling Pete has gone to God at 8.20 a.m. As dawn was
breaking in rose, purple and azure, his new dawn came. He
is with You, my beloved God, and You and he are together
with me. I've always said that love was the bonding agent
between Peter and me. And God IS love. ... Last night much
loved members of the family sat together with me and Pete
as he went through his final journey. He made little infant
sounds and sighs as his breath became shorter and shorter.
We held his lovely, frail hands, whispered to him, prayed with
him and for him. What a sad privilege. And life ebbed away
in that quiet room with so many caring people around us.
...We were given a room in which some of us rested while
others stayed awake, watching, waiting and praying. And
there were delicate, sensitive little miracles at every turn. Just
as he or we needed something, it came. And that has been so
since the beginning of this crisis. I could never, never thank
You enough. And now I know Peter is there with You. ...
Peter looked so like Christ hanging on the cross, bearded
head falling sideways, lungs straining for breath, his arms out
at his sides, noble in that last huge expression of life bridging
over the horizon to Eternity. ... My darling has gone. But
Peter, my rock, is now built into me subsumed into the Spirit
which animates me. ...When he drew his last breath, I
couldn't really believe it though I touched his cold
extremities, nose, ears and feet. I couldn't, cannot, grasp this
change in my life. Hold me, good God, as I try to emerge
onto the slippery slope. Hold me tight, give me light,
strengthen me beyond my known capabilities ... I shall
remember so many wonderful people, as well as the little
things – the blue-spotted bedspread, the tick and whirr of the
morphine machine and the drip, my pressing the relic of the
true Cross against his arm, the trill of birdsong in the dawn
outside. As Peter died...

I have emerged. I have learnt to call myself a 'widow'. It is strange when one first applies that description to oneself. In those early days, people often seemed shy to approach me on the street, sometimes crossing to the other side. I didn't feel hurt because I felt somewhat at odds with my own social capabilities too. If they felt that I might cry, I also had that anxiety. Please, I prayed, not that in the middle of the supermarket. Yet it would, of course, be so natural and understandable – healthy too. But somewhere inside myself, I didn't want to embarrass people, and I couldn't trust myself emotionally. I tried to get to the shops before the rush hours and then return home by the quietest way. By nature, I'm shy and quite unsure of myself anyway. One continues to have unexpected waves of grief. These are triggered by a memory, a place, an incident or a pair of maroon-striped swimming trunks. But most of all it is the little things that trigger sadness; coming home when there is no-one there to greet me no-one to share the 'cuppa' and a bit of local chat; no-one to sound ideas against. I never used think of nor notice the companionable silences, those times when he did the crossword as I wrote a letter. He'd share a crossword clue, or I'd ask how to spell a certain word. We had our own way of saying things, our pet-names for local characters, our shorthand for recalling events. No-one else would understand what it meant for one to say 'Chat, chat' to the other. I guess all couples have such private ways to express themselves and laugh at the little, foolish things. Certain doors just swing closed.

Certainly, in widowhood, social life changes drastically at home. When Peter retired he and I used to make instant decisions such as packing a picnic basket and catching a fleeting couple of hours of unexpected sunshine; if I had worked at my desk all morning, or had a 'low' he would suggest a bar-lunch, a 'Molly'. Perhaps, at our evening meal, we would decide to pop out to a film. Strangely, looking at something on TV, quite silent but with another person there, is different from viewing alone. I have never been to a film on my own.

Peter and I were not inclined towards big social events. Going out in a foursome is something that changes with the death of one. Couples are not always the place for a widow. Naturally I and they feel different in a threesome. Yes, I enjoy the companionship of men, but it is not easy to acquire ready-made male companionship to specification! I have a few very loyal and good men and women friends, and the family look out for me with unending and patient love. For younger widows, there is, of course, a time when another marriage may be contemplated. The right time spells itself out. But I'm a quiet person and appreciate solitude. Loneliness, I grapple with still from time to time. Self-pity. Wow! Watch it. It could drag you down the plug-hole in the bath.

One recovers. In many ways, one changes. Prayer has meant a lot to me during all this time. I have felt overcome by the mystery of life and death which comes and goes like the tide. But I have known that I could sit quietly with the Lord and tell Him exactly what is in my heart – even when there seemed to be an emptiness. Sometimes I feel wonderful consolation. Other times, nothing. When I walk, apparently alone, I walk with Him. As I wrote in that journal entry in 1998 'Peter and I were bonded by Love'. I have no need to be afraid.

I hasten to add that just as I do get times of loneliness, anxiety, depression I see these as my natural lot. Nothing is perfect and we all have negotiate the hills and hollows of life. Peter and I did that in life together. Ours was not an unending cloud nine marriage because each of us married a human being and, of course, we brought our own woundedness into our relationship. One misses the wounded companion, regrets any pain one added and rejoices in the joys and healings that were shared over the years.

I remember receiving word from a woman who whispered to me through her letter about her husband's death: 'Tell no-one, but even though I'm crying now, he was "a street angel and a home devil."' Her pain was real. So many people weep at the end of a life because it was so much less than their ideal. They had often tried so hard and, at times, given up on trying. They weep for all they struggled with. That struggle was made in a loving effort to try to make things better. Even though that woman thought that she was weeping for her lost life, for the boy and girl in love that they had been, she was also crying with the relief that all that went wrong was over now. And that is a normal reaction which is not often enough talked about with compassion. Counselling the bereaved is a blessing available to us nowadays that I hope many will avail of in such times of loss and pain. A beloved family member or close friend can be a wonderfully sensitive counsellor. Gradually we become able to move on.

Our children miss their Dad. I remember that on Christmas Day, 1977 I published a little poem in the *Sunday Press* entitled 'Today I thought of fathers':

> *Today I thought of fathers*
> *Coming in all shapes and sizes,*
> *Tall ones,*
> *Round ones,*
> *Lanky ones;*
> *Holding tiny hands*
> *Kicking football,*
> *Trying to plait little-girl hair*
> *Being Santa Claus.*
> *Today I thought of fathers*
>
> *The gifts they give,*
> *The security,*
> *The protection*
> *Being lifted up in strong arms,*
> *Mending punctures*
> *Making little boys feel big*
> *Reading bed-time stories.*

Today I thought of fathers
Those who don't feel loved
Tired ones,
Unsuccessful ones,
Whose children turn away.
Hiding behind masks
Trying not to notice
Drinking to ease pain.

Today I thought of fathers
I thought of God as Father
His gift Of Himself
Making everything possible
Knowing me by name
Being there always
So few saying 'Thank You'.

Today I thought of mothers
First cradles of children
Tender hearts,
Working at loving,
The courageous 'yes' of Mary
Joseph's protectiveness.
I thought of families
And I wanted to hug them all.

19

Survive and Move On

An identity crisis arrived with grief. 'Who am I now?' I asked myself after Peter's death 'What will be my role in life from now on?' In the months before Peter had become seriously ill, I had decided to retire from my own work. I was letting the work taper off with that in mind. Peter and I had made plans for some new things we would do on retirement. He did an unplanned new thing: he died. When Peter's condition became worse, I cancelled all my engagements. I felt myself to be in an unreal world. It was then that I read a little piece that I found so helpful: 'To need God desperately every day is a gift; waking up lonely or ill every day and putting oneself into God's tender compassionate care. That's a gift.' When I first copied out those words I was aware of the truth in them. In the darkness I said 'Thank You.' 'Who am I?' no longer presented me with a totally empty page.

I decided to move house. I knew that is not advised for a newly-bereaved person. But it seemed right for me. I wanted to be nearer my family in Dublin and I knew that a smaller house would make sense. We had been only about three years in Springfield. I had a compelling desire to turn over a new page and to try to work on a new map for my ongoing journey in life. I know people who want very strongly to hold on to memories and I understand how grieving comes in different ways for different people. I didn't find any comfort in holding on. Jesus has said 'I am going to prepare a place for you (Angela)' and that I find to be a marvellously personal promise for the future. So, since there is a place for me across the horizon, all that remains is that I follow the route there. A little sort of 'gate-lodge' would suit me meanwhile, I thought. No gate-lodge and no route came to mind just then. I had a gap to bridge.

I learned how to cry. At first I didn't want to cry when I was out. People would see me and be embarrassed. I didn't want to cry indoors either; my eyes get very red and stingy from crying and someone might call. There was also the feeling that to allow myself to cry was to lead myself into the unknown. Would I crack up altogether? My daughter Barbara, encouraged me to let the tears flow. 'Let out a long wail "Yaaahhh", if that is what you feel like, Mum. It will do you good.' she said comfortingly. She was right. After a tearful session one day I chanced to turn on the radio – any old station – and what song came up but 'There's a hundred, thousand angels by your side.' Suddenly for a few minutes the kitchen was wonderfully crowded. Little delicate gifts come our way. We need to be on the look out for them.

I knew that I needed to avoid the twin demons of boredom and self-pity. People cheerfully suggested golf and bridge. I wondered why these two occupations seemed to be recommended almost automatically even by the doctor? I'd never golfed, though golf courses are delightful places – all that open green space. I haven't the sort of personality for bridge – it's too serious for me, I'd be so concerned for my partner. I'd prefer a light-hearted game of poker! I already had things I loved doing – reading (in bed!), drawing, writing, a good play or an art exhibition, driving to the hills, the woods and the sea, savouring the beauties of nature, a soul-refreshing walk. But without Peter? (I hum 'There's a hundred thousand angels...') Not every friend is suited to that kind of outing. Long ago we went to remote and lovely places where we knew that a kingfisher would appear beside the lake or bluebells covered a glade or an ancient cemetery was crowded with daffodils. But as a single woman, I wouldn't be too happy about a very quiet spot on my own. I'm blessed with one particular friend who has a like feeling for adventure outings in search of beautiful places. But he's not in Dublin.

The house move took place four months after Pete died and was a great distraction. My new-found little dwelling has something of the character of 'gate-lodge' and was compared by a friend to a wren's nest. I like that; it suggests somewhere cosy and warm, as my little home is. I had never lived on my own before and I knew now that I wouldn't have to find a little corner for meditation as in the old family days: the whole house could be like a hermitage when I wanted that. The immediate challenge was to fit a quart into a pint bottle.

I had to do a cull on our books, my beloved books. I augmented the stocks of charity shops and auction rooms. And still I had too many things in varieties of classifications. My daughters were glad of some reminders of Dad and of the old home. But they had no time for embroidered table linen and little silver pieces. Life today is too busy for such niceties. Bit by bit, tenderly helped by my girls, my changeover was effected.

In autumn 1998 I felt dislocated and decided to return to doing some work in schools. Invitations continued to come in to me in all sorts of strange ways since few of the principals knew where I had got to. I love how the work stimulates creativity and a familiar feeling of 'neededness'. Perhaps I had mistakenly identified too strongly with my work? Friends encouraged me to go back to doing just a little.

After a year's absence, I found that the changes had accelerated – or was it that I had slowed down? On the face of it, I got on quite well because there are things about children that never change. The parents had changed more than the children. In the 1960s a lot of concern centred on what was sinful or not sinful in the area of sexuality. It was felt that sexual intercourse shouldn't be mentioned to adolescents. In the 1970s the more conservative were suggesting that condoms should not be mentioned. By 1980 the more liberal seemed to want me to make sure that their daughters would not get pregnant at an inconvenient time. Full stop. Fewer showed interest in the part that moral values, responsibilities, right and wrong played in the whole relationships and sexuality arena. 'Sin', from being an exaggerated source of anxiety, measurement and guilt, was totally disappearing from the agenda. There was however, still the feeling that parents would like me to do 'it'; not feeling confident themselves, they settled for my 'delightful little eccentricities'. Parents still find sex education a difficult subject at home. Dads in particular find it hard to talk to their sons (not to mention daughters) and often suggest 'Let him learn the way I learnt. Didn't I get on fine?' The mother, remembering, is not so sure! Some were glad that God counted on my scene and told me so. I had to learn not to talk automatically in class about 'your mum and dad' since now families come in all shapes and sizes. (Yet, children still like to have the typical family of mum, dad and siblings). Children, far from being gauche and silent, were ever ready for discussions – 'Tell us about the boys' dangly bits!'– and off we went. Laughter is a potent sharing. I had to take a disciplined role if we were not to go off on red herrings and fail to cover necessary explanations. For the first time, deep inside myself I realised that my days were numbered. I no longer had the same energy and some of the attitudes I was coming across caused me dismay and anxiety. I encouraged parents to use the two introductory Sex Education videos I and Francis McCrickard had prepared earlier in the 1990s in order to break the ground of sex education with their children at home. These are being used with ten-year-olds and their parents in quite a number of schools up to the present time.

Also, I was aware that I needed nurturing myself. Gustave Jung wrote, 'Loneliness does not result from the absence of people around us, but is experienced when people around us do not understand what is going on inside us.' My four daughters were and are wonderful friends to me, and I've nine delightful grandchildren aged from twenty-three down to seven. Lucky me!

When a new term came I again cut down on schools' work, though counselling parents was still an aspect of the work that I found to be life-giving for myself – and I hope, for the individual clients. Letters have never completely 'dried up' as old correspondents keep me informed of their life developments. I joined a couple of classes and met with friends for lunches in a way I had never been able to do so freely before. Two friends and I amused ourselves by setting up a little three-member writing group. We all love reading. We gave ourselves 'homework' and had fun reading out the results of those varied challenges. Of us, I wrote:

> *The three of them sit in a huddle*
> *There is nothing they couldn't work out,*
> *When one of them gets in a muddle*
> *The solution the others would shout.*

> *What they talk of they never give tuppence*
> *From archaeology right down to food,*
> *The Church gets its timely come-uppance,*
> *And the government – when in the mood.*

> *They don't have to make an agenda,*
> *Of which topic they couldn't care less,*
> *Over coffee and biscuits they mend a*
> *Situation, whatever the mess.*

You can see what light-hearted sharing that has been! It has suited parts of the three of us very well. We are all quite different in ways. We've all had our problems. There are, of course, people who have extrovert and buoyant personalities and can overcome upsets in a wonderful way. Peter used say "There's naught so quare as folks.'

Prayer can become a happy life-line as one grows older. For me it is contact with my Invisible Companion. Often just chatting. Some would say that isn't prayer. For me, it is. Meditation and contemplation are so comforting and yet these can be filled with the sticks and stones of distraction and restlessness. It's a matter of persevering just giving the time. Sometimes I meditate with the Taizé chants on in the background or some light, quietly flowing classical music makes way for silence. At other non-meditation times, romantic songs from the forties and fifties or songs from the 'Shows' appeal to the mood of the moment. I often dream of whirling around a ballroom as I bend and stretch with the vacuum-cleaner. A sticker on the back of a car made me smile. It read 'Angels fly because they take themselves lightly'.

'All manner of things shall be well'. It is such a gift to recognise that. There are times when the more reflective frame of mind is not available and I like to get up and get going, shaping new ideas and fresh initiatives in my head. Occasionally, not wanting to be further educated, I view a daft film. I really believe that God wants us to smile, be light-hearted and look out for fun. After all, as Julia Cameron wrote, 'Here's what I like about God: trees are crooked, mountains are lumpy, a lot of his creatures are funny-looking, and he made it all anyway.'*

Life is a river flowing between two banks – on one bank is celebrated the sublime moment of birth, the other is the adventure of death. Little by little, stepping stones are dropped in front of me as I cross the river of my life – little footholds where I can pause and find my bearings; a round stone for a wonderful family, an oblong one for an understanding friend, the jagged stone of memories, a stone big enough to sit on in the sun. I try to find positive things to do which are mini islands in the flowing river of my life. From time to time I get stuck in the clump of reeds which represent my old 'low'. From that perspective, I swopped my 'old pal' typewriter for a computer and it became the next stone to step onto – apprehensively. A Goddaughter of mine – bless you, Jilly – patiently taught me how to use it. 'Why not write a book?' I asked myself. Placing another stone ahead of me in the river, I stepped apprehensively on to new territory. It wobbled before it settled. And here I am.

* *Walking in this World*, Julia Cameron